selected
poems
E. E. CUMMINGS

selected

poems

E. E. CUMMINGS

with
introduction
and commentary
by

RICHARD S. KENNEDY

LIVERIGHT
New York

The text of this book is composed in Ehrhardt and the display set in Gill Sans Light. Composition by The Maple-Vail Book Manufacturing Group. Manufacturing by Haddon Craftsmen, Inc.
Book design by Charlotte Staub

Library of Congress Cataloging-in-Publication Data

Cummings, E. E. (Edward Estlin), 1894–1962.
[Poems. Selections]
Selected poems / E. E. Cummings ; with introduction and commentary
by Richard S. Kennedy.
p. cm.
I. Kennedy, Richard S. II. Title.
PS3505.U334A6 1994
811'.52—dc20   94-29263

ISBN 0-87140-153-3 cloth
ISBN 0-87140-154-1 paper

W. W. Norton & Company, Inc.
500 Fifth Avenue, New York, N.Y. 10110
www.wwnorton.com

W. W. Norton & Company Ltd.
Castle House, 75/76 Wells Street, London W1T 3QT
17 18 19 20

FOR JIM

who goes
his own
quiet way

CONTENTS

Other Seasons, Other Creatures

III   THE POETRY OF THE EYE   31

The Creative Process

The Cubist Break-Up

XI   TARGETS OF SATIRE   137

War

Politics

Communism and Fascism

The Literary Scene

Misanthropic Moods

XII ENDINGS 163

Self-Excoriation

Religious Leanings

Whispers of Mortality

POSTLUDE 181

Introduction

AT A POETRY READING on April 10, 1959, at Bryn Mawr College, E. E. Cummings found an auditorium crammed to the walls with young women who thrilled to his reading of "it is so long since my heart has been with yours." But whenever he read at the YM-YWHA Poetry Center in New York, which had what Cummings called his "best by much" audience, his hearers preferred his verses that were satiric attacks on politicians and generals or wiseacre accounts of sexual encounters.

These two audiences were responding to two important aspects of Cummings' work, his lyricism and his satire, but a third mode of expression, what he called his "modernist manner," was really his distinctive idiom. He developed this style because he was a painter as well as a poet. Cummings, always talented with pencil and brush, began to paint seriously while he was a junior at Harvard, shortly after seeing the Armory Show during its exhibit in Boston in 1913. He was especially enthusiastic about Marcel Duchamp's *Nude Descending a Staircase* and Constantin Brancusi's *Mademoiselle Pogany*, the two most controversial works in the show (one was derided as "an explosion in a shingle factory" and the other as "a polished egg"). The exposure to Cubism encouraged him to become a Cubist painter and also stimulated him to develop a poetic style in which he wrenched language into new meanings by way of fragmented statements, harsh juxtapositions, grammatical distortions, and startling images. "The Symbol of all Art is the Prism," he declared. "The goal is unrealism. The method is destructive. To break up the white light of objective realism into the secret glories which it contains."

Since he was a painter, he also brought a visual orientation to the placement of his poems on the page. Not only did he play with typography and punctuation marks for special effects, but he also created many poems whose full significance can be understood only when seen in their spatial arrangement on the page.

Early in his career, he became known most widely for his placing lowercase letters where capitals are expected, and especially for his use of a small "i" for personal reference. The persona he thus created represents someone who stands away from the crowd, unappreciated, without power, yet able to open his heart with song or mock the follies of society and denounce the pretensions of authority.

Because of his unusual way of handling language, Cummings had to travel a long road from the time his early books were ridiculed for their eccentricity to the point at which, with Robert Frost, he was one of the two most popular poets in America. He had, at length, taught his audience how to read him.

The poems selected for the present volume are representative of the great variety of work that brought him this fame. They range from some of his earliest creations, such as his imitation of a medieval ballad, "all in green went my love riding," which he composed for a Harvard class in "English Versification," up through such vivacious linguistic acrobatics as "r-p-o-p-h-e-s-s-a-g-r," his presentation of a grasshopper gathering itself for a leap, and on to the lurching doggerel of "THANKSGIVING (1956)," his outcry over the disastrous outcome of the Hungarian Revolution, and finally to the sonnets of his later years, such as "Now i lay(with everywhere around)," his valediction after fifty years of sonneteering. The poems display many moods: the youthful exuberance of "into the strenuous briefness," his joyous acceptance of whatever life will bring; the reflections of guilt and fear of sex, as in "the dirty colours of her kiss have just"; the cheerful description of the damnation he was willing to suffer for his beloved, in "chérie"; the depiction of the new state of self that love had brought him, in "look"; down to the misanthropic depths of "pity this busy monster,manunkind,/not"; and finally to the serenity of "in time of daffodils(who know." A number of Cummings' drawings and sketches are included in order to remind the reader of the visual perspective that he always brought to his literary work. The selection of poems gathered here, a small percentage of his prolific output, is a suitable tribute to Cummings on the one-hundredth anniversary of his birth.

E. E. Cummings at his studio window, 4 Patchin Place,
New York, photograph by David Dunham
Houghton Library, Harvard University

PRELUDE

into the strenuous briefness
Life:
handorgans and April
darkness,friends

i charge laughing.
Into the hair-thin tints
of yellow dawn,
into the women-coloured twilight

i smilingly
glide.   I
into the big vermilion departure
swim,sayingly;

(Do you think?)the
i do,world
is probably made
of roses & hello:

(of solongs and,ashes)

Ink sketch by E. E. Cummings
Houghton Library, Harvard University

1

A CHILD'S WORLD

EDWARD ESTLIN CUMMINGS had an idyllic childhood. He lived in a spacious family home where he was much loved in the midst of an extended family: parents, little sister, two grandmothers, an unmarried aunt, and a bachelor uncle—plus two servant girls and a black handyman who were also family. The Cummings home was in a quiet neighborhood in Cambridge, Massachusetts, where children's games and rituals were partly traditional and partly spontaneous. His father, Edward Cummings, a Unitarian minister and former Harvard professor, had much free time to devote to Estlin. He took him to Bostock's Animal Extravaganza, Forepaugh and Sells' Circus, and Buffalo Bill's Wild West Show. He built him a tree house that even had a little stove on which Estlin and the neighbor children could pop corn and roast marshmallows. In addition, Estlin spent blissful summer months at Joy Farm in Silver Lake, New Hampshire, where his father taught him woodcraft and nature lore and in the evening his mother, Rebecca Cummings, read aloud to the family from Scott, Dickens, and Stevenson. His mother hoped that he would become a poet like Mr. Longfellow, *whose spirit lingered on in Cambridge. She encouraged him to keep a journal and to write verses from the time he was a little boy.*

The memory of these happy days live on in many poems that he wrote throughout his career, some of which are included in this section. In his first volume of verse, Tulips and Chimneys, he called them "Chansons Innocentes," taking the title from a group of Debussy piano pieces. The best known of these, "in Just-," began, in an early version, as an exercise in free verse for his Harvard class in "English Versification." He was always able to identify with children and even with animals—as the prose poem "at the head of this street a gasping organ" makes clear. The form is one of many he tried in 1919 in imitation of Mallarmé.

As time went on, he wrote a number of poems in the rhythmic patterns and nonsense phrasing of nursery rhymes. "o by the by" and "if everything happens that can't be done" come from his book 1 x 1, which was published in the midst of World War II in 1944. The joyous theme of that book is oneness, especially oneness in love, but the expressions of joy in life that emanate from the nursery rhymes are important contributions to his purpose, as he said, "of trying to cheer up my native land." But Cummings could also give a satirical edge to his nonsense rhymes as is evident in "as freedom is a breakfastfood." Yet even when he is displaying an awareness of darkness and doom—as dire as world catastrophe—he still can emerge with an optimistic outlook, as in "what if a much of a which of a wind." An innocent optimism was so basic to his nature that no discouragements or fits of depression could smother it, and it bursts forth at some point in every book of poetry that he published.

Days of Innocence

1

who are you,little i

(five or six years old)
peering from some high

window;at the gold

of november sunset

(and feeling:that if day
has to become night

this is a beautiful way)

2

in Just-
spring   when the world is mud-
luscious the little
lame balloonman

whistles   far   and wee

and eddieandbill come
running from marbles and
piracies and it's
spring

when the world is puddle-wonderful

the queer
old balloonman whistles
far   and   wee
and bettyandisbel come dancing

from hop-scotch and jump-rope and

it's
spring
and
    the

       goat-footed

balloonMan   whistles
far
and
wee

3

who sharpens every dull
here comes the only man
reminding with his bell
to disappear a sun

and out of houses pour
maids mothers widows wives
bringing this visitor
their very oldest lives

one pays him with a smile
another with a tear

some cannot pay at all
he never seems to care

he sharpens is to am
he sharpens say to sing
you'd almost cut your thumb
so right he sharpens wrong

and when their lives are keen
he throws the world a kiss
and slings his wheel upon
his back and off he goes

but we can hear him still
if now our sun is gone
reminding with his bell
to reappear a moon

4

O the sun comes up-up-up in the opening

sky(the all the
any merry every pretty each

bird sings birds sing
gay-be-gay because today's today)the
romp cries i and the me purrs

you and the gentle
who-horns says-does moo-woo
(the prance with the
three white its stimpstamps)

the grintgrunt wugglewiggle
champychumpchomps yes
the speckled strut begins to scretch and
scratch-scrutch

and scritch(while
the no-she-yes-he fluffies tittle
tattle did-he-does-she)& the

ree ray rye roh
rowster shouts

rawrOO

5

maggie and milly and molly and may
went down to the beach(to play one day)

and maggie discovered a shell that sang
so sweetly she couldn't remember her troubles,and

milly befriended a stranded star
whose rays five languid fingers were;

and molly was chased by a horrible thing
which raced sideways while blowing bubbles:and

may came home with a smooth round stone
as small as a world and as large as alone.

For whatever we lose(like a you or a me)
it's always ourselves we find in the sea

at the head of this street a gasping organ is waving moth-eaten
tunes.   a fattish hand turns the crank;the box spouts fairies,out
of it sour gnomes tumble clumsily,the little box is spilling ran-
cid elves upon neat sunlight into the flowerstricken air which is
filthy with agile swarming sonal creatures

—Children,stand with circular frightened faces glaring at the
shabby tiny smiling,man in whose hand the crank goes desperately,
round and round pointing to the queer monkey

(if you toss him a coin he will pick it cleverly from,the air and
stuff it seriously in,his minute pocket)Sometimes he does not
catch a piece of money and then his master will yell at him over
the music and jerk the little string and the monkey will sit,up,
and look at,you with his solemn blinky eyeswhichneversmile and
after he has caught a,penny or three,pennies he will be thrown a
peanut(which he will open skilfully with his,mouth carefully
holding,it,in his little toylike hand)and then he will stiff-ly
throw the shell away with a small bored gesture that makes the
children laugh.

But i don't,   the crank goes round desperate elves and hopeless
gnomes and frantic fairies gush clumsily from the battered box
fattish and mysterious the flowerstricken sunlight is thickening
dizzily is reeling gently the street and the children and the mon-
keyandtheorgan and the man are dancing slowly are tottering up
and down in a trembly mist of atrocious melody....tiniest dead
tunes crawl upon my face my hair is lousy with mutilated singing
microscopic things in my ears scramble faintly tickling putres-
cent atomies,
                    and
                         i feel the jerk of the little string!the tiny
smiling shabby man is yelling over the music i understand him i
shove my round red hat back on my head i sit up and blink at you
with my solemn eyeswhichneversmile

yes,By god.
for i am they are pointing at the queer monkey with a little
oldish doll-like face and hairy arms like an ogre and rubbercolour-
ed hands and feet filled with quick fingers and a remarkable tail
which is allbyitself alive.(and he has a little red coat with i
have a real pocket in it and the round funny hat with a big feather
is tied under myhis chin.)   that climbs and cries and runs and
floats like a toy on the end of a string

7

who were so dark of heart they might not speak,
a little innocence will make them sing;
teach them to see who could not learn to look
—from the reality of all nothing

will actually lift a luminous whole;
turn sheer despairing to most perfect gay,
nowhere to here,never to beautiful:
a little innocence creates a day.

And something thought or done or wished without
a little innocence,although it were
as red as terror and as green as fate,
greyly shall fail and dully disappear—

but the proud power of himself death immense
is not so as a little innocence

Adult Nursery Rhymes

I

o by the by
has anybody seen
little you-i
who stood on a green
hill and threw
his wish at blue

with a swoop and a dart
out flew his wish
(it dived like a fish
but it climbed like a dream)
throbbing like a heart
singing like a flame

blue took it my
far beyond far
and high beyond high
bluer took it your
but bluest took it our
away beyond where

what a wonderful thing
is the end of a string
(murmurs little you-i
as the hill becomes nil)
and will somebody tell
me why people let go

2

if everything happens that can't be done
(and anything's righter
than books
could plan)
the stupidest teacher will almost guess
(with a run
skip
around we go yes)
there's nothing as something as one

one hasn't a why or because or although
(and buds know better
than books
don't grow)
one's anything old being everything new
(with a what
which
around we come who)
one's everyanything so

so world is a leaf so tree is a bough
(and birds sing sweeter
than books
tell how)
so here is away and so your is a my
(with a down
up
around again fly)
forever was never till now

now i love you and you love me
(and books are shuter
than books
can be)
and deep in the high that does nothing but fall
(with a shout

each
around we go all)
there's somebody calling who's we

we're anything brighter than even the sun
(we're everything greater
than books
might mean)
we're everyanything more than believe
(with a spin
leap
alive we're alive)
we're wonderful one times one

3

as freedom is a breakfastfood
or truth can live with right and wrong
or molehills are from mountains made
—long enough and just so long
will being pay the rent of seem
and genius please the talentgang
and water most encourage flame

as hatracks into peachtrees grow
or hopes dance best on bald men's hair
and every finger is a toe
and any courage is a fear
—long enough and just so long
will the impure think all things pure
and hornets wail by children stung

or as the seeing are the blind
and robins never welcome spring

nor flatfolk prove their world is round
nor dingsters die at break of dong
and common's rare and millstones float
—long enough and just so long
tomorrow will not be too late

worms are the words but joy's the voice
down shall go which and up come who
breasts will be breasts thighs will be thighs
deeds cannot dream what dreams can do
—time is a tree(this life one leaf)
but love is the sky and i am for you
just so long and long enough

4

what if a much of a which of a wind
gives the truth to summer's lie;
bloodies with dizzying leaves the sun
and yanks immortal stars awry?
Blow king to beggar and queen to seem
(blow friend to fiend:blow space to time)
—when skies are hanged and oceans drowned,
the single secret will still be man

what if a keen of a lean wind flays
screaming hills with sleet and snow:
strangles valleys by ropes of thing
and stifles forests in white ago?
Blow hope to terror;blow seeing to blind
(blow pity to envy and soul to mind)
—whose hearts are mountains,roots are trees,
it's they shall cry hello to the spring

what if a dawn of a doom of a dream
bites this universe in two,
peels forever out of his grave
and sprinkles nowhere with me and you?
Blow soon to never and never to twice
(blow life to isn't:blow death to was)
—all nothing's only our hugest home;
the most who die,the more we live

5

when faces called flowers float out of the ground
and breathing is wishing and wishing is having—
but keeping is downward and doubting and never
—it's april(yes,april;my darling)it's spring!
yes the pretty birds frolic as spry as can fly
yes the little fish gambol as glad as can be
(yes the mountains are dancing together)

when every leaf opens without any sound
and wishing is having and having is giving—
but keeping is doting and nothing and nonsense
—alive;we're alive,dear:it's(kiss me now)spring!
now the pretty birds hover so she and so he
now the little fish quiver so you and so i
(now the mountains are dancing,the mountains)

when more than was lost has been found has been found
and having is giving and giving is living—
but keeping is darkness and winter and cringing
—it's spring(all our night becomes day)o,it's spring!
all the pretty birds dive to the heart of the sky
all the little fish climb through the mind of the sea
(all the mountains are dancing;are dancing)

Mount Chocorua, watercolor painting by E. E. Cummings
SUNY College at Brockport Foundation
Photograph courtesy of the E. E. Cummings Trust

II

SWEET SPONTANEOUS
EARTH

THE RETURN OF SPRING for the Cummings family was always greeted with the joy that is common to New Englanders after the rigors of winter. Even as a small child, Estlin recorded the flowering of the first crocus in his journal. In his later years, springtime in New York met with his welcome, as the ailanthus tree ("tree of heaven") came into leaf outside his third-floor studio window at 4 Patchin Place. In 1920, the year of his first appearance in a major literary magazine, the Dial, he printed five poems devoted to spring, including "spring omnipotent goddess" (his father did not approve of those slobbering thighs) and "O sweet spontaneous earth."

Cummings was indebted to his boyhood summers at Joy Farm for his Wordsworthian love of nature. The stacks of juvenile verse that continued to pile up during his years at the Cambridge Latin School are interlaced with poems on songbirds, hawks, chipmunks, butterflies, sunsets, moonrises, and misty dawns.

In his adult life, after the death of his father in 1926, Cummings continued to live at Joy Farm from May to October every year, and the place became an increasingly satisfying retreat in the years after World War II, for New York had changed from a very livable city to an overpopulated, traffic-snarled center of urban hustle. He took up birdwatching and thumbed well Roger Tory Peterson's guidebooks. He painted Mount Chocorua as often as Cézanne did Mont Sainte-Victoire. Watching the sun set behind the mountain became an evening ritual that he required everyone in the house to join.

The poems in this section show many moods as well as individual responses to spring, birds, mountains, sunrise, and sunset. But most of them come from the early period when Cummings sought imagery that brought surprise, such as in "beyond the stolid iron pond," in which he presented sunrise in terms of judging a harvest competition and then of a gambler on a roll, or in "the sky a silver," in which the rain is likened to a Debussy piano piece and the mist to a game of blindman's buff. Or they display his Cubist diction, as in "beyond the brittle towns asleep" with its "chattering sunset" and its "stealing needles of foam" "threading" the shore.

In all periods of his writing Cummings shows his delight in the rhythms of the seasons. No experience of the natural scene could bring him more lift of heart than looking out his window to watch fluttering snowflakes, as he depicts them in "SNO," sounding like tiny angels stropping themselves against flower petals. But when winter had ruled for months, he was ready to push back the cold and say hello to spring.

Spring

I

spring omnipotent goddess thou dost
inveigle into crossing sidewalks the
unwary june-bug and the frivolous angleworm
thou dost persuade to serenade his
lady the musical tom-cat,thou stuffest
the parks with overgrown pimply
cavaliers and gumchewing giggly
girls and not content
Spring,with this
thou hangest canary-birds in parlor windows

spring slattern of seasons you
have dirty legs and a muddy
petticoat,drowsy is your
mouth your eyes are sticky
with dreams and you have
a sloppy body
from being brought to bed of crocuses
When you sing in your whiskey-voice
                                    the grass
rises on the head of the earth
and all the trees are put on edge

spring,
of the jostle of
thy breasts and the slobber
of your thighs
i am so very
               glad that the soul inside me Hollers
for thou comest and your hands
are the snow
and thy fingers are the rain,

and i hear
the screech of dissonant
flowers,and most of all
i hear your stepping

                    freakish feet
                    feet incorrigible
ragging the world,

2

O sweet spontaneous
earth how often have
the
doting

      fingers of
prurient philosophers pinched
and
poked

thee
,has the naughty thumb
of science prodded
thy

    beauty   .how
often have religions taken
thee upon their scraggy knees
squeezing and

buffeting thee that thou mightest conceive
gods
    (but
true

to the incomparable
couch of death thy
rhythmic
lover

    thou answerest

them only with

        spring)

3

  in

  Spring comes(no-
  one
  asks his name)

  a mender
  of things

  with eager
  fingers(with
  patient
  eyes)re

  -new-

  ing remaking what
  other
  -wise we should

19

have
thrown a-

way(and whose

brook
-bright flower-
soft bird
-quick voice loves

children
and sunlight and

mountains)in april(but
if he should
Smile)comes

nobody'll know

4

Spring is like a perhaps hand
(which comes carefully
out of Nowhere)arranging
a window,into which people look(while
people stare
arranging and changing placing
carefully there a strange
thing and a known thing here)and

changing everything carefully

spring is like a perhaps
Hand in a window
(carefully to
and fro moving New and
Old things,while
people stare carefully
moving a perhaps
fraction of flower here placing
an inch of air there)and

without breaking anything.

5

the sky a silver
dissonance by the correct
fingers of April
resolved

                into a
clutter of trite jewels

now like a moth with stumbling

wings flutters and flops along the
grass collides with trees and
houses and finally,
butts into the river

now winging selves sing sweetly,while ghosts(there
and here)of snow cringe;dazed an earth shakes sleep
out of her brightening mind:now everywhere
space tastes of the amazement which is hope

gone are those hugest hours of dark and cold
when blood and flesh to inexistence bow
(all that was doubtful's certain,timid's bold;
old's youthful and reluctant's eager now)

anywhere upward somethings yearn and stir
piercing a tangled wrack of wishless known:
nothing is like this keen(who breathes us)air
immortal with the fragrance of begin

winter is over—now(for me and you,
darling!)life's star prances the blinding blue

Other Seasons, Other Creatures

I

SNO

a white idea(Listen

drenches:earth's ugly)mind.
,Rinsing with exact death

the annual brain
                        clotted with loosely voices
look
look.   Skilfully

.fingered by(a parenthesis
the)pond on whoseswooning edge

black trees think

(hear little knives of flower
stropping sof a.   Thick silence)

blacktreesthink

tiny,angels sharpen:themselves

(on
    air)
don't speak
                A white idea,

drenching.   earth's brain detaches
clottingsand from a a nnual(ugliness

of)rinsed mind slowly:

from!the:A wending putrescence.   a.of,loosely

;voices

2

beyond the stolid iron pond
soldered with complete silence
the huge timorous hills
squat like permanent vegetables

the judging sun pinches smiling
here and there some huddling vastness
claps the fattest finally
and tags it with his supreme blue

whereat the just adjacent valley
rolls proudly his belligerent bosom
deepens his greens inflates his ochres
and in the pool doubles his winnings

3

the hills
like poets put on
purple thought against
the

24

magnificent clamor of

                         day

tortured
in gold,which presently

crumpled
collapses
exhaling a red soul into the dark

so
duneyed master
enter
the sweet gates

                         of my heart and

take
the
rose,

which perfect
is
With killing hands

4

beyond the brittle towns asleep
i look where stealing needles of foam
in the last light

thread the creeping shores

as out of dumb strong hands infinite

the erect deep upon me
in the last light
pours its eyeless miles

the chattering sunset ludicrously
dies,i hear only tidewings

in the last light
twitching at the world

5

may my heart always be open to little
birds who are the secrets of living
whatever they sing is better than to know
and if men should not hear them men are old

may my mind stroll about hungry
and fearless and thirsty and supple
and even if it's sunday may i be wrong
for whenever men are right they are not young

and may myself do nothing usefully
and love yourself so more than truly
there's never been quite such a fool who could fail
pulling all the sky over him with one smile

6

now comes the good rain farmers pray for(and
no sharp shrill shower bouncing up off
burned earth but a blind blissfully seething
gift wandering deeply through godthanking ground)

bluest whos of this snowy head we call
old frank go bluer still as(shifting his life
from which to which)he reaches the barn's immense
doorway and halts propped on a pitchfork(breathing)

lovers like rej and lena smile(while looming
darkly a kindness of fragrance opens around
them)and whisper their joy under entirely the coming
quitenotimaginable silenceofsound

(here is that rain awaited by leaves with all
their trees and by forests with all their mountains)

7

a wind has blown the rain away and blown
the sky away and all the leaves away,
and the trees stand.   I think i too have known
autumn too long

          (and what have you to say,
wind wind wind—did you love somebody
and have you the petal of somewhere in your heart
pinched from dumb summer?
                O crazy daddy
of death dance cruelly for us and start

the last leaf whirling in the final brain
of air!)Let us as we have seen see
doom's integration.........a wind has blown the rain

away and the leaves and the sky and the
trees stand:
                the trees stand.   The trees,
suddenly wait against the moon's face.

8

mouse)Won
derfully is
anyone else entirely who doesn't
move(Moved more suddenly than)whose

tiniest smile?may Be
bigger than the fear of all
hearts never which have
(Per

haps)loved(or than
everyone that will Ever love)we
've
hidden him in A leaf

and,
Opening
beautiful earth
put(only)a Leaf among dark

ness.sunlight's
thenlike?now
Disappears
some

thing(silent:
madeofimagination
;the incredible soft)ness
(his ears(eyes

9

when god lets my body be

From each brave eye shall sprout a tree
fruit that dangles therefrom

the purpled world will dance upon
Between my lips which did sing

a rose shall beget the spring
that maidens whom passion wastes

will lay between their little breasts
My strong fingers beneath the snow

Into strenuous birds shall go
my love walking in the grass

their wings will touch with her face
and all the while shall my heart be

With the bulge and nuzzle of the sea

Sound, oil painting by E. E. Cummings
Metropolitan Museum, New York
Photograph courtesy of the E. E. Cummings Trust

III

THE POETRY OF THE EYE

AFTER CUMMINGS HAD DISCOVERED Cubism and Futurism (the Italian painter Marinetti's term for Cubism in motion), he read all that he could on the new developments in the arts. Later, when he enrolled in the Norton-Harjes Ambulance Corps and was sent to France in 1917 as an ambulance driver, he found the modern movement in the arts flourishing in Paris. He saw Stravinsky's ballet *Pétrouchka*, staged by Les Ballets Russes. He attended the première of Erik Satie's *Parade* with sets by Picasso. He visited the Luxembourg Gallery, where the paintings of the Impressionists and Cézanne, a precursor of Cubism, were on display. He was able to buy Matisse prints at the stalls of the *bouquinistes*. All this exposure to new concepts in art made its impact on the experiments that Cummings began to try out. He had recognized the key feature of the new art, which was *break-up and restructuring*. Although Cubism provided the initial impulse that pushed him toward new directions in literary expression, he continued to be innovative for decades, in the same way that Cubism as an international style in the visual arts developed into other modes on the way to abstraction.

31

The first four poems in this section show Cummings' attempt to express his inner experience in the creation of a literary or an artistic work. The first one, "of my," written before 1920, conveys his sense of entering a new world of aesthetic expression where the forms and motifs of the modern French painters exist. The second, also written before 1920, is a tribute to Picasso in which he tries to express in words what Picasso achieved in line and color.

The second group of poems in this section shows the effects that the new painters had on Cummings' work. "writhe and," begun in 1916, presents sunset in the city: it first depicts the harshness of the cityscape by means of twisted and distorted word usage and through images of noise—breaking, scraping, colliding, shouts and crashes. Then the language changes the angularity of the city buildings, softening them into natural forms as dusk falls.

The emphasis here and in "Picasso" is on sound, but the rest of the poems in this group depend on visual arrangements. Generally speaking, Cummings' handling of spacing, typography, and punctuation provides visual guidance in most of his poems. But here is a cluster of poems that go further. In order for a reader to experience these works at all, they must be seen on the page. In fact, they cannot be read aloud.

In "mr. smith," we see on the left side of the page a man sitting by the fireside reading a letter, the handwriting of which is described in the middle of the page, and then we read phrases from the letter on the right side of the page. His response to the letter, "smiles friend smith" and "haha" are in mid-page, joining the two sides. As we come to understand from the fragments of the letter that it is a tearful message from a girl whose mother has insisted on breaking up their relationship, we feel pathos the more keenly because of the comfortable picture of "mr. smith" warming his toes that has been built up on the left side of the page. More important, the visual arrangement, including the fragmented contents of the letter, has required the reader to participate in bringing the poem into meaning.

Patterns are the main feature of many of these poems. "the sky" is an experiment in arranging words in columns according to their vowel sounds. The poem "n" has its symmetry of letters and letter groups, very appropriate for its quiet theme. The others show action. "l(a" presents a statement about a falling leaf in an arrangement that brings out the idea of oneness embedded in loneliness. The remainder of the poems give visual presentation to whatever is being stated or described: a green sprout growing, a grasshopper leaping, an electrical storm, a foggy dawn, a striptease dancer moving through her routine, birds in flight that disappear, Sunday morning bells ringing.

Cummings had in mind creations of this sort when he said, 'The day of the spoken lyric is past. The poem which has at last taken its place does not sing itself; it builds itself, three-dimensionally, gradually, subtly, in the consciousness of the experiencer."

The Creative Process

I

of my
soul a street is:
prettinesses Pic-
abian tricktrickclickflick-er
garnished
of stark Picasso
throttling trees

hither
my soul
repairs herself with
prisms of sharp mind
and Matisse rhythms
to juggle Kandinsky gold-fish

away from the gripping gigantic
muscles of Cézanne's
logic,
        oho.
        a street
there is

where strange birds   purr

2

Picasso
you give us Things
which
bulge:grunting lungs pumped full of sharp thick mind

you make us shrill
presents always
shut in the sumptuous screech of
simplicity

(out of the
black unbunged
Something gushes vaguely a squeak of planes
or

between squeals of
Nothing grabbed with circular shrieking tightness
solid screams whisper.)
Lumberman of The Distinct

your brain's
axe only chops hugest inherent
Trees of Ego,from
whose living and biggest

bodies lopped
of every
prettiness

you hew form truly

The Cubist Break-Up

I

writhe and
gape of tortured

  perspective
  rasp and graze of splintered

normality
            crackle and
            sag
  of planes   clamors of
  collision
  collapse   As

peacefully,
lifted
into the awful beauty
                    of sunset

                    the young city
putting off dimension with a blush
enters
the becoming garden of her agony

2

mr. smith
is reading
his letter
by the fire-
light

    tea-time

        smiles friend smith

no type   bold o's
         d's gloat
         droll l's twine
         r's rove

        haha

           sweet-hearts
           part   fellow
           like   darl- write
           i dream my   try ned   ma
           thinks
           right thing   will be still
           till death
           thine

blows ring

strokes nose   P
toasts toes   S
             kiss

3

                the sky
                was   can dy
        lu   mi
                nous   ed
                            i
                ble
                    spry   pinks
                    shy   lem
                ons

                                    greens
            cool
        choco   lates
                un   der
    a   lo
            co
            mo   tive   s pout
                            ing
                    vi
            o   lets

4

l(a

le
af
fa

ll

s)
one
l

iness

5

s(

these out of in
finite no
where,who;arrive s
trollingly

:alight whitely and.

)now
flakes:are;guests,of t
wi
ligh

t

6

how

tinily
of

squir(two be
tween sto
nes)ming a gr

eenes
t you b
ecome

s whi
(mysterious
ly)te

one
t

hou

7

n
OthI
n

g can

s
urPas
s

the m

y
SteR
y

of

s
tilLnes
s

8

r-p-o-p-h-e-s-s-a-g-r
                    who
a)s w(e loo)k
upnowgath
            PPEGORHRASS
                          eringint(o-
aThe):l
        eA
          !p:
S   a
            (r
rIvInG   .gRrEaPsPhOs)
                                    to
rea(be)rran(com)gi(e)ngly
,grasshopper;

9

n(o)w

        the
how
      dis(appeared cleverly)world

iS Slapped:with;liGhtninG
!

  at
which(shal)lpounceupcrackw(ill)jumps

of
   THuNdeRB
          loSSo!M iN
-visiblya mongban(gedfrag-
ment ssky?wha tm)eani ngl(essNessUn
rolli)ngl yS troll s(who leO v erd)oma insCol

Lide.!high
           n , o ; w :
                         theraIncomIng

o all the roofs roar
                drownInsound(
&
(we(are like)dead
)Whoshout(Ghost)atOne(voiceless)O
ther or im)
   pos
   sib(ly as
   leep)
      But l!ook—
         s

   U

      n:starT birDs(lEAp)Openi ng
t hing ; s(
—sing
)all are aLl(cry alL See)o(ver All)Th(e grEEn

?eartH)N,ew

as if as

if a mys
teriouSly("i am alive"

)
 brave

ly and(th
e moon's al-down)most whis
per(here)ingc r O

wing;ly:cry.be,gi N s agAains

t b
ecomin
gsky?t r e e s
!

m ore&(o uto f)mor e torn(f og r

e
elingwhiRls)are pouring rush fields drea
mf(ull

          y

             are.)
&
som

ewhereishbudofshape

now,s
tI
r
ghost

?s

tirf lic;k

e rsM-o
:ke(c.
    l

i,

m
 !
b
)& it:s;elf,

mmamakmakemakesWwOwoRworLworlD

       | |

    sh estiffl
    ystrut sal
    lif san
    dbut sth

    epouting(gWh.ono:w
    s li psh ergo
    wnd ow n,
            r
    Eve

    aling 2 a
    -sprout eyelands)sin
    uously&them&twi
    tching,begins

    unununun?
    butbutbut??
      tonton??
    ing????

—Out-&
          steps;which
flipchucking
.grins
gRiNdS

d is app ea r in gly
eyes grip live loop croon mime
nakedly hurl asquirm the
dip&giveswoop&swoon&ingly

seethe firm swirl hips whirling climb to
GIVE
(yoursmine mineyours yoursmine
!
i()t)

12

birds(
　　　here,inven
ting air
U
)sing

tw
iligH(
t's
　　v
　　　va
　　　　vas
　vast

ness.Be)look
now
　　(come
soul;
&:and

who
　　s)e
　　　　voi
c
es
(
　are
　　ar
　　　a

(b
  eLl
     s?
       bE

-ginningly(come-swarm:faces
ar;rive go.faces a(live)
sob bel
ls

(pour wo
       (things)
             men
                selves-them

inghurl)bangbells(yawnchurches
suck people)reel(dark-
ly(whirling
in

(b
  ellSB
      el
        Ls)

-to sun(crash).Streets
glit
ter
a,strut:do;colours;are:m,ove

o im
    -pos-
       sibl
           y

(ShoutflowereD
flowerish boom

b el Lsb El l
s!cry)

(be
    llsbe
        lls)
            b
            (be
                llsbell)
                    ells
                        (sbells)

Rebecca H. Cummings, pencil sketch by E. E. Cummings
Houghton Library, Harvard University

IV

PORTRAITS

CUMMINGS' PORTRAITS VARY in tone. He is reverent in associating his mother with a flower garden and his father with an individualistic strength, but most of his characterizations are touched with criticism. His group portrait of "the Cambridge ladies" finds their minds metaphorically cluttered with shabby and mismatched objects like a furnished room for rent. The ladies have no more knowledge of the charitable causes they support than they have appreciation of natural beauty, since the moon is as attractive to them as the last uneaten chocolate in the candy box. The views of Buffalo Bill and Joe Gould are a mixture of admiration and condescension. "Buffalo Bill's" conveys a nostalgic hero worship tempered by an adult view of him as a showman. Actually, Cummings had a secret respect for Joe Gould, a Harvard graduate who lived the life of a homeless man in Greenwich Village. He saw Gould as an urban Thoreau, ready to experience the primitive life of the streets and to seek only what was essential for survival.

The last poem in this section is an elegy for Sam Ward, a New Hampshire handyman who looked after Joy Farm during the winter and carried out repairs in the summer, a scarcely literate man of laconic speech but solid character and one whom Cummings valued as a strong, unique individual. Cummings has skillfully worked in a number of Sam's phrases in order to convey his New Hampshire coloration and his acceptance of life, whatever it would bring, including the "what" of afterlife.

the Cambridge ladies who live in furnished souls
are unbeautiful and have comfortable minds
(also,with the church's protestant blessings
daughters,unscented shapeless spirited)
they believe in Christ and Longfellow,both dead,
are invariably interested in so many things—
at the present writing one still finds
delighted fingers knitting for the is it Poles?
perhaps.   While permanent faces coyly bandy
scandal of Mrs. N and Professor D
....the Cambridge ladies do not care,above
Cambridge if sometimes in its box of
sky lavender and cornerless,the
moon rattles like a fragment of angry candy

2

if there are any heavens my mother will(all by herself)have
one.   It will not be a pansy heaven nor
a fragile heaven of lilies-of-the-valley but
it will be a heaven of blackred roses

my father will be(deep like a rose
tall like a rose)

standing near my

swaying over her
(silent)
with eyes which are really petals and see

nothing with the face of a poet really which
is a flower and not a face with
hands
which whisper
This is my beloved my

                                (suddenly in sunlight
he will bow,

& the whole garden will bow)

                              3

my father moved through dooms of love
through sames of am through haves of give,
singing each morning out of each night
my father moved through depths of height

this motionless forgetful where
turned at his glance to shining here;
that if(so timid air is firm)
under his eyes would stir and squirm

newly as from unburied which
floats the first who,his april touch
drove sleeping selves to swarm their fates
woke dreamers to their ghostly roots

and should some why completely weep
my father's fingers brought her sleep:
vainly no smallest voice might cry
for he could feel the mountains grow.

Lifting the valleys of the sea
my father moved through griefs of joy;
praising a forehead called the moon
singing desire into begin

joy was his song and joy so pure
a heart of star by him could steer
and pure so now and now so yes
the wrists of twilight would rejoice

keen as midsummer's keen beyond
conceiving mind of sun will stand,
so strictly(over utmost him
so hugely)stood my father's dream

his flesh was flesh his blood was blood:
no hungry man but wished him food;
no cripple wouldn't creep one mile
uphill to only see him smile.

Scorning the pomp of must and shall
my father moved through dooms of feel;
his anger was as right as rain
his pity was as green as grain

septembering arms of year extend
less humbly wealth to foe and friend
than he to foolish and to wise
offered immeasurable is

proudly and(by octobering flame
beckoned)as earth will downward climb,
so naked for immortal work
his shoulders marched against the dark

his sorrow was as true as bread:
no liar looked him in the head;

if every friend became his foe
he'd laugh and build a world with snow.

My father moved through theys of we,
singing each new leaf out of each tree
(and every child was sure that spring
danced when she heard my father sing)

then let men kill which cannot share,
let blood and flesh be mud and mire,
scheming imagine,passion willed,
freedom a drug that's bought and sold

giving to steal and cruel kind,
a heart to fear,to doubt a mind,
to differ a disease of same,
conform the pinnacle of am

though dull were all we taste as bright,
bitter all utterly things sweet,
maggoty minus and dumb death
all we inherit,all bequeath

and nothing quite so least as truth
—i say though hate were why men breathe—
because my father lived his soul
love is the whole and more than all

4

Buffalo Bill 's
defunct
    who used to
    ride a watersmooth-silver
             stallion
and break onetwothreefourfive pigeonsjustlikethat
                       Jesus

he was a handsome man
               and what i want to know is
how do you like your blueeyed boy
Mister Death

5

little joe gould has lost his teeth and doesn't know where
to find them(and found a secondhand set which click)little
gould used to amputate his appetite with bad brittle
candy but just(nude eel)now little joe lives on air

Harvard Brevis Est for Handkerchief read Papernapkin no laundry
bills likes People preferring Negroes Indians Youse
n.b. ye twang of little joe(yankee)gould irketh sundry
who are trying to find their minds(but never had any to lose)

and a myth is as good as a smile but little joe gould's quote oral
history unquote might(publishers note)be entitled a wraith's
progress or mainly awash while chiefly submerged or an amoral
morality sort-of-aliveing by innumerable kind-of-deaths

(Amérique Je T'Aime and it may be fun to be fooled
but it's more fun to be more to be fun to be little joe gould)

6

rain or hail
sam done
the best he kin
till they digged his hole

:sam was a man

stout as a bridge
rugged as a bear
slickern a weazel
how be you

(sun or snow)

gone into what
like all them kings
you read about
and on him sings

a whippoorwill;

heart was big
as the world aint square
with room for the devil
and his angels too

yes,sir

what may be better
or what may be worse
and what may be clover
clover clover

(nobody'll know)

sam was a man
grinned his grin
done his chores
laid him down.

Sleep well

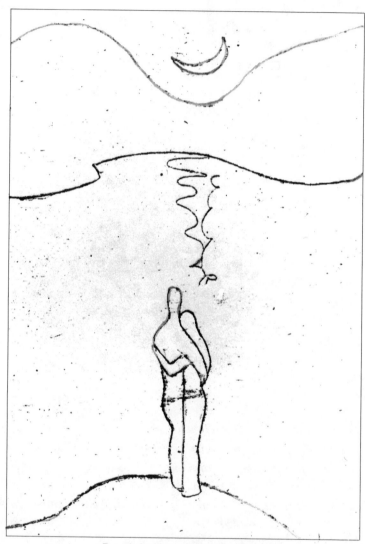

Pencil sketch by E. E. Cummings
Houghton Library, Harvard University

V

LOVE AND ITS MYSTERIES

DURING THE COURSE of his lifetime, Cummings was married
to three of the most beautiful women in America, and most
of his love poems are addressed to them. From 1919 to 1924,
his emotions were centered on the demure Elaine Orr, whom
he married after her divorce from his friend Scofield Thayer.
From 1925 to 1932, he was devoted to Anne Barton, former
wife of the illustrator Ralph Barton and a lively and witty
fashion model, who became his second wife. From 1932 until
his death in 1962, he lived happily with Marion Morehouse,
an actress, photographer, and fashion model, whom the pho-
tographer Edward Steichen judged to have been the most
outstanding of all the women who had ever posed for him.

The love poems vary in attitude. The restraint of "O Dis-
tinct" derives from Cummings' self-conscious aim to be dif-
ferent from the traditional troubadour. But the sophisticated
view of the Last Judgment and Hell in "chérie" does not
detract from its controlled emotional statement that the
speaker is ready to suffer damnation for his love. "along the
brittle treacherous bright streets" reflects an authentic emo-
tion of longing after an extended separation from Elaine when

she was across the sea. The delicate floral metaphors of "somewhere i have never travelled," which make it one of the most intense of Cummings' works in his early style, were a tribute to Anne Barton. All but one of the last six in this section were written for Marion Morehouse and there is no literary posturing in them. Their directness, their play with the concept of oneness, and their emphasis on the linguistic affirmation of "yes" gives these poems an unstrained sincerity.

I

O Distinct
Lady of my unkempt adoration
if i have made
a fragile certain

song under the window of your soul
it is not like any songs
(the singers the others
they have been faithful

to many things and which
die
i have been sometimes true
to Nothing and which lives

they were fond of the handsome
moon   never spoke ill of the
pretty stars   and to
the serene the complicated

and the obvious
they were faithful
and which i despise,
frankly

admitting i have been true
only to the noise of worms.
in the eligible day
under the unaccountable sun)

Distinct Lady
swiftly take
my fragile certain song
that we may watch together

how behind the doomed
exact smile of life's
placid obscure palpable
carnival where to a normal

melody of probable violins dance
the square virtues and the oblong sins
perfectly
gesticulate the accurate

strenuous lips of incorruptible
Nothing   under the ample
sun,under the insufficient
day under the noise of worms

2

my love is building a building
around you,a frail slippery
house,a strong fragile house
(beginning at the singular beginning

of your smile)a skilful uncouth
prison,a precise clumsy
prison(building thatandthis into Thus,
Around the reckless magic of your mouth)

my love is building a magic,a discrete
tower of magic and(as i guess)

when Farmer Death(whom fairies hate)shall

crumble the mouth-flower fleet
He'll not my tower,
                        laborious,casual

where the surrounded smile
                        hangs

                                breathless

somewhere i have never travelled,gladly beyond
any experience,your eyes have their silence:
in your most frail gesture are things which enclose me,
or which i cannot touch because they are too near

your slightest look easily will unclose me
though i have closed myself as fingers,
you open always petal by petal myself as Spring opens
(touching skilfully,mysteriously)her first rose

or if your wish be to close me,i and
my life will shut very beautifully,suddenly,
as when the heart of this flower imagines
the snow carefully everywhere descending;

nothing which we are to perceive in this world equals
the power of your intense fragility:whose texture
compels me with the colour of its countries,
rendering death and forever with each breathing

(i do not know what it is about you that closes
and opens;only something in me understands
the voice of your eyes is deeper than all roses)
nobody,not even the rain,has such small hands

4

chérie
        the very,picturesque,last Day
(when all the clocks have lost their jobs and god
sits up quickly to judge the Big Sinners)
he will have something large and fluffy to say
to me.   All the pale grumbling wings

of his greater angels will cease:as that Curse

bounds neat-ly from the angry wad

of his forehead(then fiends with pitchforkthings
will catch and toss me lovingly to
and fro.)   Last,should you look,you
'll find me prone upon a greatest flame,

which seethes in a beautiful way
upward;with someone by the name
of Paolo passing the time of day.

5

along the brittle treacherous bright streets
of memory comes my heart,singing like
an idiot,whispering like a drunken man

who(at a certain corner,suddenly)meets
the tall policeman of my mind.
                              awake
being not asleep,elsewhere our dreams began
which now are folded:but the year completes
his life as a forgotten prisoner

—"Ici?"—"Ah non,mon chéri;il fait trop froid"—
they are gone:along these gardens moves a wind bringing
rain and leaves,filling the air with fear
and sweetness....pauses.   (Halfwhispering....halfsinging

stirs the always smiling chevaux de bois)

when you were in Paris we met here

6

you shall above all things be glad and young.
For if you're young,whatever life you wear

it will become you;and if you are glad
whatever's living will yourself become.
Girlboys may nothing more than boygirls need:
i can entirely her only love

whose any mystery makes every man's
flesh put space on;and his mind take off time

that you should ever think,may god forbid
and(in his mercy)your true lover spare:
for that way knowledge lies,the foetal grave
called progress,and negation's dead undoom.

I'd rather learn from one bird how to sing
than teach ten thousand stars how not to dance

7

yes is a pleasant country:
if's wintry
(my lovely)
let's open the year

both is the very weather
(not either)
my treasure,
when violets appear

love is a deeper season
than reason;
my sweet one
(and april's where we're)

8

it is so long since my heart has been with yours

shut by our mingling arms through
a darkness where new lights begin and
increase,
since your mind has walked into
my kiss as a stranger
into the streets and colours of a town—

that i have perhaps forgotten
how,always(from
these hurrying crudities
of blood and flesh)Love
coins His most gradual gesture,

and whittles life to eternity

—after which our separating selves become museums
filled with skilfully stuffed memories

9

your homecoming will be my homecoming—

my selves go with you,only i remain;
a shadow phantom effigy or seeming

(an almost someone always who's noone)

a noone who,till their and your returning,
spends the forever of his loneliness
dreaming their eyes have opened to your morning

feeling their stars have risen through your skies:

so,in how merciful love's own name,linger
no more than selfless i can quite endure
the absence of that moment when a stranger
takes in his arms my very life who's your

—when all fears hopes beliefs doubts disappear.
Everywhere and joy's perfect wholeness we're

10

one's not half two.   It's two are halves of one:
which halves reintegrating,shall occur
no death and any quantity;but than
all numerable mosts the actual more

minds ignorant of stern miraculous
this every truth—beware of heartless them
(given the scalpel,they dissect a kiss;
or,sold the reason,they undream a dream)

one is the song which fiends and angels sing:
all murdering lies by mortals told make two.
Let liars wilt,repaying life they're loaned;
we(by a gift called dying born)must grow

deep in dark least ourselves remembering
love only rides his year.
                                        All lose,whole find

11

silently if,out of not knowable
night's utmost nothing,wanders a little guess
(only which is this world)more my life does
not leap than with the mystery your smile

sings or if(spiralling as luminous
they climb oblivion)voices who are dreams,
less into heaven certainly earth swims
than each my deeper death becomes your kiss

losing through you what seemed myself,i find
selves unimaginably mine;beyond
sorrow's own joys and hoping's very fears

yours is the light by which my spirit's born:
yours is the darkness of my soul's return
—you are my sun,my moon,and all my stars

12

hate blows a bubble of despair into
hugeness world system universe and bang
—fear buries a tomorrow under woe
and up comes yesterday most green and young

pleasure and pain are merely surfaces
(one itself showing,itself hiding one)
life's only and true value neither is
love makes the little thickness of the coin

comes here a man would have from madame death
neverless now and without winter spring?

she'll spin that spirit her own fingers with
and give him nothing(if he should not sing)

how much more than enough for both of us
darling.   And if i sing you are my voice,

13

being to timelessness as it's to time,
love did no more begin than love will end;
where nothing is to breathe to stroll to swim
love is the air the ocean and the land

(do lovers suffer?all divinities
proudly descending put on deathful flesh:
are lovers glad?only their smallest joy's
a universe emerging from a wish)

love is the voice under all silences,
the hope which has no opposite in fear;
the strength so strong mere force is feebleness:
the truth more first than sun more last than star

—do lovers love?why then to heaven with hell.
Whatever sages say and fools,all's well

Charcoal sketch by E. E. Cummings
Houghton Library, Harvard University

VI

ACHIEVING THE
TOGETHERCOLOURED
INSTANT

DURING HIS CAREER, Cummings was well known for the frank celebration of sexual intercourse in his work. Yet he exercised a good deal of wit and skill in keeping these poems from descending into pornography, using wordplay, allusion, parody, extended metaphor, spacing, and form to deflect their erotic impact. Some are in sonnet form, a stanzaic arrangement that had been used for love poems ever since Petrarch. But toward the end of the Elizabethan period, Shakespeare introduced a contrasting approach with his "dark lady" sonnets, an anti-Petrarchan tradition that Cummings follows in "my girl's tall," with its play back and forth with "long hard" and "hard long" in the octave and the tough-minded vine imagery in the sestet. "O It's Nice To Get Up In,the slipshod mucous kiss" depends upon an allusion that most readers are unfamiliar with. It refers to a popular song that Harry Lauder rendered in his rich Scottish burr in the British music halls:

> Oh, it's nice to get up in the morning
> When the sun is beginning to shine,
> And it's three or four or five o'clock
> In the good old summer time . . .

"(ponder,darling,these busted statues" is a hard-grained item in the carpe diem tradition, with its echoes of Andrew Marvell's "To His Coy Mistress." "she being Brand" is a comic treatment that pokes fun, too, at the American male's love affair with the automobile.

The last four poems in this section are more serious and more direct in their handling. The dialogue of former lovers meeting in "think of it:not so long ago" builds in nostalgic stages toward its conclusion. All of the next three develop the theme of a new sense of self that is attained in sexual union. The last of them, "i like my body when it is with your," in its delicacy of statement and its simplicity of repeated phrasing, stands as the best erotic poem Cummings ever wrote.

my girl's tall with hard long eyes
as she stands,with her long hard hands keeping
silence on her dress,good for sleeping
is her long hard body filled with surprise
like a white shocking wire,when she smiles
a hard long smile it sometimes makes
gaily go clean through me tickling aches,
and the weak noise of her eyes easily files
my impatience to an edge—my girl's tall
and taut,with thin legs just like a vine
that's spent all of its life on a garden-wall,
and is going to die.   When we grimly go to bed
with these legs she begins to heave and twine
about me,and to kiss my face and head.

2

O It's Nice To Get Up In,the slipshod mucous kiss
of her riant belly's fooling bore
—When The Sun Begins To(with a phrasing crease
of hot subliminal lips,as if a score
of youngest angels suddenly should stretch neat necks
just to see how always squirms
the skilful mystery of Hell)me suddenly

grips in chuckles of supreme sex.

In The Good Old Summer Time.
My gorgeous bullet in tickling intuitive flight
aches,just,simply,into,her.   Thirsty
stirring. (Must be summer.   Hush.   Worms.)

But It's Nicer To Lie In Bed
                        —eh?   I'm

not.   Again.   Hush.   God.   Please hold.   Tight

                        3

        (ponder,darling,these busted statues
        of yon motheaten forum be aware
        notice what hath remained
        —the stone cringes
        clinging to the stone,how obsolete

        lips utter their extant smile....
        remark

        a few deleted of texture
        or meaning monuments and dolls

        resist Them Greediest Paws of careful
        time all of which is extremely
        unimportant)whereas Life

        matters if or

        when the your- and my-
        idle vertical worthless
        self unite in a peculiarly
        momentary

        partnership(to instigate
        constructive
                        Horizontal
        business....even so,let us make haste

—consider well this ruined aqueduct

lady,
which used to lead something into somewhere)

4

she being Brand

-new;and you
know consequently a
little stiff i was
careful of her and(having

thoroughly oiled the universal
joint tested my gas felt of
her radiator made sure her springs were O.

K.)i went right to it flooded-the-carburetor cranked her

up,slipped the
clutch(and then somehow got into reverse she
kicked what
the hell)next
minute i was back in neutral tried and

again slo-wly;bare,ly nudg.   ing(my

lev-er Right-
oh and her gears being in
A 1 shape passed
from low through
second-in-to-high like
greasedlightning)just as we turned the corner of Divinity

avenue i touched the accelerator and give

her the juice,good

(it

was the first ride and believe i we was
happy to see how nice she acted right up to
the last minute coming back down by the Public
Gardens i slammed on

the
internalexpanding
&
externalcontracting
brakes Bothatonce and

brought allofher tremB
-ling
to a:dead.

stand-
;Still)

5

n w
O
h
S
LoW
h
myGODye
s s

6

"think of it:not so long ago
this was a village"

               "yes;i know"

"of human beings who prayed and sang:
or am i wrong?"

                 "no,you're not wrong"

"and worked like hell six days out of seven"
"to die as they lived:in the hope of heaven"

"didn't two roads meet here?"

                    "they did;
and over yonder a schoolhouse stood"

"do i remember a girl with blue-
sky eyes and sun-yellow hair?"

                     "do you?"

"absolutely"

         "that's very odd,
for i've never forgotten one frecklefaced lad"

"what could have happened to her and him?"
"maybe they waked and called it a dream"

"in this dream were there green and gold
meadows?"

              "through which a lazy brook strolled"

"wonder if clover still smells that way;
up in the mow"

              "full of newmown hay"

"and the shadows and sounds and silences"
"yes,a barn could be a magical place"

"nothing's the same:is it"

"something still
remains,my friend;and always will"

"namely?"
"if any woman knows,
one man in a million ought to guess"

"what of the dreams that never die?"
"turn to your left at the end of the sky"

"where are the girls whose breasts begin?"
"under the boys who fish with a pin"

7

look
my fingers,which
touched you
and your warmth and crisp
littleness
—see?do not resemble my
fingers.   My wrists hands
which held carefully the soft silence
of you(and your body
smile eyes feet hands)
are different
from what they were.   My arms
in which all of you lay folded
quietly,like a
leaf or some flower
newly made by Spring
Herself,are not my
arms.   I do not recognise
as myself this which i find before
me in a mirror.   i do
not believe
i have ever seen these things;

someone whom you love
and who is slenderer
taller than
myself has entered and become such
lips as i use to talk with,
a new person is alive and
gestures with my
or it is perhaps you who
with my voice
are
playing.

8

sometimes i am alive because with
me her alert treelike body sleeps
which i will feel slowly sharpening
becoming distinct with love slowly,
who in my shoulder sinks sweetly teeth
until we shall attain the Springsmelling
intense large togethercoloured instant

the moment pleasantly frightful

when,her mouth suddenly rising,wholly
begins with mine fiercely to fool
(and from my thighs which shrug and pant
a murdering rain leapingly reaches the
upward singular deepest flower which she
carries in a gesture of her hips)

i like my body when it is with your
body.   It is so quite new a thing.
Muscles better and nerves more.
i like your body.   i like what it does,
i like its hows.   i like to feel the spine
of your body and its bones,and the trembling
-firm-smooth ness and which i will
again and again and again
kiss,   i like kissing this and that of you,
i like,slowly stroking the,shocking fuzz
of your electric fur,and what-is-it comes
over parting flesh....And eyes big love-crumbs,

and possibly i like the thrill

of under me you so quite new

VII

KITTY, MIMI, MARJ, AND FRIENDS

LIKE ANY NORMAL young fellow, Cummings was fascinated with sex in his early years, but since he was a minister's son growing up surrounded by the repressive Puritanism of Cambridge, Massachusetts, he had plenty of fear and trepidation about this hush-hush subject. Even so, his fascination continued to increase in his late teens and early twenties when he brushed close to commercial sex in Boston or New York. But his attitude toward the prostitutes he saw, heard about, or even talked to was ambiguous—like that of the "clever drolls" in the poem "kitty" who "keep their sunday flower."

When he was shipped to France as a driver for the Norton-Harjes Ambulance Corps in 1917, he was surprised to find an open and unselfconscious attitude toward sex among the French. During their month in Paris, he and his friend Slater Brown struck up acquaintance with two beautiful prostitutes, Marie Louise Lallemand and her sidekick, Mimi, whom they dined with and escorted about in the same way they would treat American dates. His poem "little ladies more," with its collage of the street invitations and chatter of the prostitutes, reflects this Parisian sojourn.

Charcoal sketch by E. E. Cummings
Houghton Library, Harvard University

But Cummings was still too apprehensive about venereal disease to engage in any intercourse with Marie Louise, in spite of the fact that on one occasion he spent the night with her. It was not until he had been imprisoned in a French detention camp for four months (see his book *The Enormous Room* for an account of this ordeal) that his apprehensions about sex disappeared. Upon release, he sought Marie Louise in Paris but could not find her. Finally, on the day before he sailed back to the United States, he had his first complete sexual experience with a waitress in a couscous restaurant, who took him home for the night. He was twenty-three years old at the time.

During the next year, while he was in the army at Camp Devens, Massachusetts, he wrote a great many poems about prostitutes, usually in sonnet form, which he delighted in using because his subject matter stood in such high contrast to the sonnet tradition. Actually, Cummings was not a sexually promiscuous person nor one who patronized prostitutes, although he knew a good deal about them from his living in Greenwich Village before and after his adventures in France. He was "a one-woman man," according to Slater Brown, and at the time he wrote most of these poems he was carrying on a love affair with Elaine Thayer. But in these poems about the sex trade, Cummings reveled in being a source of shock to his contemporaries by striking an iconoclastic pose, and he enjoyed disturbing the proprieties of the Boston-Cambridge world of his father.

The poems themselves seesaw in their attitudes. Some of them display disgust or revulsion in their imagery: "her hair was like a gas/ evil to feel," or "the dirty colours of her kiss." Others imply regret or a deglamorized morning after: "Dead stars stink. dawn. Inane,/ the poetic carcass of a girl," or "she picked wearily something from the floor/ Her hair was mussed, and she coughed while tying strings." Yet still other poems show an honest appreciation for what these women provide, for instance, the praise that the working men whose "fingers toss trunks/ shuffle sacks spin kegs" have for Marj's "cleancornered strokable/ body," or the speaker's confession that Marjorie's "fragrance hurls/ me into tears." Moreover, there is no mistaking the warm remembrance that emanates from the poems with a Parisian setting.

Quite frequently, the poems feature surprise or humor, and the care that went into the sound and wordplay makes them distinctive works. Although they contributed to Cummings' early reputation as a Peck's Bad Boy of poetry, these literary creations are memorable for more than their shock value.

I

      wanta
      spendsix

      dollars Kid
              2 for the room
  and
              four   for the girl
      thewoman wasnot

      quite Fourteen   till she smiled
                                then

Centuries   she
                    soft ly
    repeated
    well   whadyas ay
          dear
          wan
          taspend

        six

      Dollars

2

twentyseven bums give a prostitute the once
-over. fiftythree(and one would see if it could)

eyes say the breasts look very good:
firmlysquirmy with a slight jounce,

thirteen pants have a hunch

admit in threedimensional distress
these hips were made for Horizontal Business
(set on big legs nice to pinch

assiduously which justgraze
each other).   As the lady lazily struts
                                        (her
thickish flesh superior to the genuine daze
of unmarketable excitation,

whose careless movements carefully scatter

pink propaganda of annihilation

3

goodby Betty,don't remember me
pencil your eyes dear and have a good time
with the tall tight boys at Tabari'
s,keep your teeth snowy,stick to beer and lime,
wear dark,and where your meeting breasts are round
have roses darling,it's all i ask of you—
but that when light fails and this sweet profound
Paris moves with lovers,two and two
bound for themselves,when passionately dusk
brings softly down the perfume of the world
(and just as smaller stars begin to husk
heaven)you,you exactly paled and curled

with mystic lips take twilight where i know:
proving to Death that Love is so and so.

4

little ladies more
than dead exactly dance
in my head,precisely
dance where danced la guerre.

Mimi à
la voix fragile
qui chatouille Des
Italiens

the putain with the ivory throat
Marie Louise Lallemand
n'est-ce pas que je suis belle
chéri? les anglais m'aiment
tous,les américains
aussi...."bon dos,bon cul de Paris"(Marie
Vierge
Priez
Pour
Nous)

with the
long lips of
Lucienne which dangle
the old men and hot
men se promènent
doucement le soir(ladies

accurately dead les anglais
sont gentils et les américains
aussi,ils payent bien les américains dance

exactly in my brain voulez-
vous coucher avec
moi? Non? pourquoi?)

ladies skilfully
dead precisely dance
where has danced la
guerre j'm'appelle
Manon,cinq rue Henri Monnier
voulez-vous coucher avec moi?
te ferai Mimi
te ferai Minette,
dead exactly dance
si vous voulez
chatouiller
mon lézard ladies suddenly
j'm'en fous des nègres

                  (in the twilight of Paris
Marie Louise with queenly
legs cinq rue Henri
Monnier a little love
begs,Mimi with the body
like une boîte à joujoux,want nice sleep?
toutes les petites femmes exactes
qui dansent toujours in my
head dis-donc,Paris

ta gorge mystérieuse
pourquoi se promène-t-elle,pourquoi
éclate ta voix
fragile couleur de pivoine?)
                     with the

long lips of Lucienne which
dangle the old men and hot men
precisely dance in my head
ladies carefully dead

5

"kitty". sixteen,5′1″,white,prostitute.

ducking always the touch of must and shall,
whose slippery body is Death's littlest pal,

skilled in quick softness. Unspontaneous. cute.

the signal perfume of whose unrepute
focusses in the sweet slow animal
bottomless eyes importantly banal,

Kitty. a whore. Sixteen
                  you corking brute
amused from time to time by clever drolls
fearsomely who do keep their sunday flower.
The babybreasted broad "kitty" twice eight

—beer nothing,the lady'll have a whiskey-sour—

whose least amazing smile is the most great
common divisor of unequal souls.

6

the poem her belly marched through me as
one army.   From her nostrils to her feet

she smelled of silence.   The inspired cleat

of her glad leg pulled into a sole mass
my separate lusts
                her hair was like a gas
evil to feel.   Unwieldy....

                              the bloodbeat
in her fierce laziness tried to repeat
a trick of syncopation Europe has

—. One day i felt a mountain touch me where
i stood (maybe nine miles off).   It was spring

sun-stirring.   sweetly to the mangling air
muchness of buds mattered.   a valley spilled
its tickling river in my eyes,
                              the killed

world wriggled like a twitched string.

                              7

when you rang at Dick Mid's Place
the madam was a bulb stuck in the door.
a fang of wincing gas showed how
hair,in two fists of shrill colour,
clutched the dull volume of her tumbling face
scribbled with a big grin. her sow-
eyes clicking mischief from thick lids.
the chunklike nose on which always the four
tablets of perspiration erectly sitting.
—If they knew you at Dick Mid's
the three trickling chins began to traipse
into the cheeks "eet smeestaire steevensun
kum een,dare ease Bet,an Leelee,an dee beeg wun"
her handless wrists did gooey severe shapes.

8

nearer:breath of my breath:take not thy tingling
limbs from me:make my pain their crazy meal
letting thy tigers of smooth sweetness steal
slowly in dumb blossoms of new mingling:
deeper:blood of my blood:with upwardcringing
swiftness plunge these leopards of white dream
in the glad flesh of my fear:more neatly ream
this pith of darkness:carve an evilfringing
flower of madness on gritted lips
and on sprawled eyes squirming with light insane
chisel the killing flame that dizzily grips.

Querying greys between mouthed houses curl

thirstily.   Dead stars stink.   dawn.   Inane,

the poetic carcass of a girl

9

the dirty colours of her kiss have just
throttled
          my seeing blood,her heart's chatter

riveted a weeping skyscraper

in me

     i bite on the eyes' brittle crust
(only feeling the belly's merry thrust
Boost my huge passion like a business

and the Y her legs panting as they press

proffers its omelet of fluffy lust)
at six exactly
                  the alarm tore

two slits in her cheeks.   A brain peered at the dawn.
she got up

            with a gashing yellow yawn
and tottered to a glass bumping things.
she picked wearily something from the floor

Her hair was mussed,and she coughed while tying strings

                        10

    in making Marjorie god hurried
    a boy's body on unsuspicious
    legs of girl. his left hand quarried
    the quartzlike face. his right slapped
    the amusing big vital vicious
    vegetable of her mouth.
    Upon the whole he suddenly clapped
    a tiny sunset of vermouth
    -colour.   Hair. he put between
    her lips a moist mistake,whose fragrance hurls
    me into tears,as the dusty new-
    ness of her obsolete gaze begins to.   lean....
    a little against me,when for two
    dollars i fill her hips with boys and girls

| |

between the breasts
of bestial
Marj lie large
men who praise

Marj's cleancornered strokable
body   these men's
fingers toss trunks
shuffle sacks spin kegs they

curl
loving
around
beers

        the world has
these men's hands but their
bodies big and boozing
belong to

Marj
the greenslim purse of whose
face opens
on a fatgold

grin
hooray
hoorah for the large
men who lie

between the breasts
of bestial Marj
for the strong men
who

sleep between the legs of Lil

Pencil sketch by E. E. Cummings,
drawn from Honoré Daumier's painting "The Washer Woman."
Houghton Library, Harvard University

VIII

THE DIMENSIONS OF
BEING HUMAN

VERY EARLY in his career, Cummings developed a personal philosophy of life that places him in the American Romantic tradition. He became a representative of the Transcendentalist school of Emerson, Thoreau, and Whitman. The earliest aspect of this position to emerge was aesthetic. From reading in art criticism and listening to the discourses of his mentor, Scofield Thayer, Cummings developed an impressionistic idea of beauty as dependent on the intensity of the viewer's or reader's response.

He carried this proposition over into all areas of life, placing primary emphasis on feeling rather than thinking: he maintained that to be "Alive" was to live at heightened emotional intensity and, conversely, that merely to exist was the equivalent of being "dead." The state of being alive he acquainted with verbs; being dead, with nouns. Thus, he valued spontaneity, creativity, whole-hearted participation in life's many tasks, and continual alertness to whatever was new and unusual but also to what was natural rather than artificial. In *The Enormous Room*, Chapter 9, he set down the first grammatical metaphor of his personal philosophy:

There are certain things in which one is unable to believe for the simple reason that he never ceases to feel them. Things of this sort—things which are always inside of us and in fact are us and which consequently will never be pushed off or away where we can begin thinking about them—are no longer things;they,and the us which they are,equals A Verb; an IS.

This is the foundation for Cummings' Romantic view of life: his preference for emotion over reason, the natural life rather than the civilized life with all its complexities, the unspoiled innocence of children rather than the sophistication of adults, what can be sensed in place of what can be measured, mystery rather than certainty, poetry rather than science. He carried this further to hold that a man who lives according to these lights is guided by his inner self, which is unique to him, and he must resist conformity to the demands of society or the state or religious orthodoxy and avoid all groups, political parties, and associations lest he lose this individual uniqueness. "How I hated my father," Cummings remembered, "for making me read Emerson's 'Self-Reliance.' Now it is my Bible."

The poems in this section present these views, which are well adapted to expressing the experience of love, the courage to face death (which is, after all, a condition of the unknown), and, in general, the grounds for living.

I

since feeling is first
who pays any attention
to the syntax of things
will never wholly kiss you;

wholly to be a fool
while Spring is in the world

my blood approves,
and kisses are a better fate
than wisdom
lady i swear by all flowers.   Don't cry
—the best gesture of my brain is less than
your eyelids' flutter which says

we are for each other:then
laugh,leaning back in my arms
for life's not a paragraph

And death i think is no parenthesis

2

all ignorance toboggans into know
and trudges up to ignorance again:
but winter's not forever,even snow
melts;and if spring should spoil the game,what then?

all history's a winter sport or three:
but were it five,i'd still insist that all
history is too small for even me;
for me and you,exceedingly too small.

Swoop(shrill collective myth)into thy grave
merely to toil the scale to shrillerness
per every madge and mabel dick and dave
—tomorrow is our permanent address

and there they'll scarcely find us(if they do,
we'll move away still further:into now

3

the trick of finding what you didn't lose
(existing's tricky:but to live's a gift)
the teachable imposture of always
arriving at the place you never left

(and i refer to thinking)rests upon
a dismal misconception;namely that
some neither ape nor angel called a man
is measured by his quote eye cue unquote.

Much better than which,every woman who's
(despite the ultramachinations of
some loveless infraworld)a woman knows;
and certain men quite possibly may have

shall we say guessed?"
                              "we shall" quoth gifted she:
and played the hostess to my morethanme

4

there are so many tictoc
clocks everywhere telling people
what toctic time it is for
tictic instance five toc minutes toc
past six tic

Spring is not regulated and does
not get out of order nor do
its hands a little jerking move
over numbers slowly

              we do not
wind it up it has no weights
springs wheels inside of
its slender self no indeed dear
nothing of the kind.

(So,when kiss Spring comes
we'll kiss each kiss other on kiss the kiss
lips because tic clocks toc don't make
a toctic difference
to kisskiss you and to
kiss me)

5

what time is it?it is by every star
a different time,and each most falsely true;
or so subhuman superminds declare

—nor all their times encompass me and you:

when are we never,but forever now
(hosts of eternity;not guests of seem)
believe me,dear,clocks have enough to do

without confusing timelessness and time.

Time cannot children,poets,lovers tell—
measure imagine,mystery,a kiss
—not though mankind would rather know than feel;

mistrusting utterly that timelessness

whose absence would make your whole life and my
(and infinite our)merely to undie

6

wherelings whenlings
(daughters of ifbut offspring of hopefear
sons of unless and children of almost)
never shall guess the dimension of

him whose
each
foot likes the
here of this earth

whose both
eyes
love
this now of the sky

—endlings of isn't
shall never

begin
to begin to

imagine how(only are shall be were
dawn dark rain snow rain
-bow &
a

moon
's whis-
per
in sunset

or thrushes toward dusk among whippoorwills or
tree field rock hollyhock forest brook chickadee
mountain.   Mountain)
whycoloured worlds of because do

not stand against yes which is built by
forever & sunsmell
(sometimes a wonder
of wild roses

sometimes)
with north
over
the barn

7

conceive a man,should he have anything
would give a little more than it away

(his autumn's winter being summer's spring
who moved by standing in november's may)
from whose(if loud most howish time derange

the silent whys of such a deathlessness)
remembrance might no patient mind unstrange
learn(nor could all earth's rotting scholars guess
that life shall not for living find the rule)

and dark beginnings are his luminous ends
who far less lonely than a fire is cool
took bedfellows for moons mountains for friends

—open your thighs to fate and(if you can
withholding nothing)World,conceive a man

8

sonnet entitled how to run the world)

A always don't there B being no such thing
for C can't casts no shadow D drink and

E eat of her voice in whose silence the music of spring
lives F feel opens but shuts understand
G gladly forget little having less

with every least each most remembering
H highest fly only the flag that's furled

(sestet entitled grass is flesh or swim
who can and bathe who must or any dream
means more than sleep as more than know means guess)

I item i immaculately owe
dying one life and will my rest to these

children building this rainman out of snow

9

dying is fine)but Death

?o
baby
i

wouldn't like

Death if Death
were
good:for

when(instead of stopping to think)you

begin to feel of it,dying
's miraculous
why?be

cause dying is

perfectly natural;perfectly
putting
it mildly lively(but

Death

is strictly
scientific
& artificial &

evil & legal)

we thank thee
god
almighty for dying

(forgive us,o life!the sin of Death

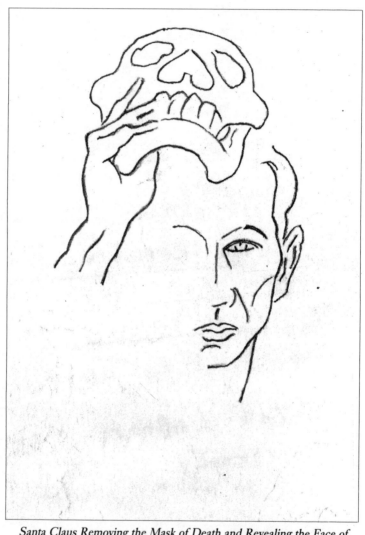

Santa Claus Removing the Mask of Death and Revealing the Face of a Young Man, pencil sketch by E. E. Cummings, 1946, intended as an illustration for *Santa Claus* but not used by the publisher
Houghton Library, Harvard University

IX

MYTHS AND ALLEGORIES

As A MINISTER, E. E. Cummings' father, Edward Cummings, frequently made use of little homemade parables in his sermons. It was, one may suppose, a manifestation of the emblematic habit of mind that was characteristic of New England before the twentieth century. Not only was Estlin exposed to all this in his earlier years, but also as a classics major at Harvard, he became steeped in Greek myths. Further, in his other studies he frequently encountered literary allegory—in a year-long course in Dante, another in Chaucer, and a semester course in "The Nature and History of Allegory." Thus, this way of thinking came easily to him.

The poems this section show a good deal of creative variety in this mode of composition. The most important of them, "anyone lived in a pretty how town," develops the central myth of Cummings' life and is closely related to the persona he created for himself, the nonhero "i." He uses the nursery-rhyme form appropriate to the world of innocence he wished to depict and tells the story of the powerless but happy "anyone," who is isolated from other people, the "someones" who are all negative in their activities and standardized in their behavior. But anyone is loved by a woman named "noone," who joins him in his response to life, no matter whether good or bad events befall. Her name allows Cummings to express both the isolation that anyone feels and the love the woman offers: "noone loved him more by more." This same doubleness applies to the response to anyone's death: "one day anyone died i guess/ (and noone stooped to kiss his face)." The poem ends with the people of the world following their fruitless routines, as anyone and noone lie buried together absorbed into the natural world and its cycle of seasons.

The next poem, "the Noster was a ship of swank," is a forthright allegorical assertion of Cummings' personal and political philosophy. It sets forth the proposition that collectivism (Noster), rationalism (Ergo), and religious authority (Pater) all fail in the presence of individualism (Sum).

The third poem is another treatment of the creative process. Cummings turns his personal philosophy into a myth of the creative urges and ideas that fall into consciousness like snowflakes onto the earth.

The rest of the myths (including a variation on the Garden of Eden story) and allegories are easy to comprehend and need no commentary except for the two based on Greek myths that may not be familiar to everyone. The first, "in heavenly realms of hellas dwelt," is an updated retelling of the story of Ares (Mars) and Aphrodite (Venus), the wife of Hephaestus (Vulcan), the smith, who surprises the pair in their love tryst. Cummings adapts the story to his accounting for the woes of modern life because of the triumph of Science. The second poem, "Tumbling-hair," is more subtle: it presents an allusive episode in the abduction of Persephone (Proserpine) by Hades (Pluto) when he finds her picking flowers in the meadow and carries her off to the Underworld.

anyone lived in a pretty how town
(with up so floating many bells down)
spring summer autumn winter
he sang his didn't he danced his did.

Women and men(both little and small)
cared for anyone not at all
they sowed their isn't they reaped their same
sun moon stars rain

children guessed(but only a few
and down they forgot as up they grew
autumn winter spring summer)
that noone loved him more by more

when by now and tree by leaf
she laughed his joy she cried his grief
bird by snow and stir by still
anyone's any was all to her

someones married their everyones
laughed their cryings and did their dance
(sleep wake hope and then)they
said their nevers they slept their dream

stars rain sun moon
(and only the snow can begin to explain
how children are apt to forget to remember
with up so floating many bells down)

one day anyone died i guess
(and noone stooped to kiss his face)
busy folk buried them side by side
little by little and was by was

all by all and deep by deep
and more by more they dream their sleep

noone and anyone earth by april
wish by spirit and if by yes.

Women and men(both dong and ding)
summer autumn winter spring
reaped their sowing and went their came
sun moon stars rain

2

the Noster was a ship of swank
(as gallant as they come)
until she hit a mine and sank
just off the coast of Sum

precisely where a craft of cost
the Ergo perished later
all hands(you may recall)being lost
including captain Pater

3

one(Floatingly)arrive

(silent)one by(alive)
from(into disappear

and perfectly)nowhere
vivid anonymous
mythical guests of Is

unslowly more who(and
here who there who)descend
-ing(mercifully)touch
deathful earth's any which

Weavingly now one by
wonder(on twilight)they
come until(over dull

all nouns)begins a whole
verbal adventure to

illimitably Grow

4

All in green went my love riding
on a great horse of gold
into the silver dawn.

four lean hounds crouched low and smiling
the merry deer ran before.

Fleeter be they than dappled dreams
the swift sweet deer
the red rare deer.

Four red roebuck at a white water
the cruel bugle sang before.

Horn at hip went my love riding
riding the echo down
into the silver dawn.

four lean hounds crouched low and smiling
the level meadows ran before.

Softer be they than slippered sleep
the lean lithe deer
the fleet flown deer.

Four fleet does at a gold valley
the famished arrow sang before.

Bow at belt went my love riding
riding the mountain down
into the silver dawn.

four lean hounds crouched low and smiling
the sheer peaks ran before.

Paler be they than daunting death
the sleek slim deer
the tall tense deer.

Four tall stags at a green mountain
the lucky hunter sang before.

All in green went my love riding
on a great horse of gold
into the silver dawn.

four lean hounds crouched low and smiling
my heart fell dead before.

5

here is little Effie's head
whose brains are made of gingerbread
when the judgment day comes
God will find six crumbs

stooping by the coffinlid
waiting for something to rise
as the other somethings did—
you imagine His surprise

bellowing through the general noise
Where is Effie who was dead?
—to God in a tiny voice,
i am may the first crumb said

whereupon its fellow five
crumbs chuckled as if they were alive
and number two took up the song,
might i'm called and did no wrong

cried the third crumb,i am should
and this is my little sister could
with our big brother who is would
don't punish us for we were good;

and the last crumb with some shame
whispered unto God,my name
is must and with the others i've
been Effie who isn't alive

just imagine it I say
God amid a monstrous din
watch your step and follow me
stooping by Effie's little,in

(want a match or can you see?)
which the six subjunctive crumbs
twitch like mutilated thumbs:
picture His peering biggest whey

coloured face on which a frown
puzzles,but I know the way—

(nervously Whose eyes approve
the blessed while His ears are crammed

with the strenous music of
the innumerable capering damned)
—staring wildly up and down
and here we are now judgment day

cross the threshold have no dread
lift the sheet back in this way.
here is little Effie's head
whose brains are made of gingerbread

6

the wind is a Lady with
bright slender eyes(who

moves)at sunset
and who—touches—the
hills without any reason

(i have spoken with this
indubitable and green person "Are
You the wind?" "Yes" "why do you touch flowers
as if they were unalive,as

if They were ideas?" "because,sir
things which in my mind blossom will
stumble beneath a clumsiest disguise,appear
capable of fragility and indecision

—do not suppose these
without any reason and otherwise
roses and mountains
different from the i am who wanders

imminently across the renewed world"
to me said the)wind being A lady in a green
dress,who;touches:the fields
(at sunset)

7

death(having lost)put on his universe
and yawned:it looks like rain
(they've played for timelessness
with chips of when)
that's yours;i guess
you'll have to loan me pain
to take the hearse,
see you again.

Love(having found)wound up such pretty toys
as themselves could not know:
the earth tinily whirls;
while daisies grow
(and boys and girls
have whispered thus and so)
and girls with boys
to bed will go,

8

don't get me wrong oblivion
I never loved you kiddo
you that was always sticking around

                    spoiling me for everyone else
                    telling me how it would make
                    you nutty if I didn't let you
                    go the distance
and I gave you my breasts to feel
didn't I
      and my mouth to kiss

   O I was too good to you oblivion old kid   that's all
   and when I might have told you
                    to go ahead and croak yourselflike
                    you was always threatening you was
                    going to do
                            I didn't
                            I said   go on you inter-
                            est me
                            I let you hang around
                            and whimper
   and I've been getting mine
Listen

there's a fellow I love like I never loved anyone else that's six
   foot two tall with a face any girl would die to kiss and a skin
   like a little kitten's
that's asked me to go to Murray's tonight with him and see the cab-
   aret and dance   you know
well
if he asks me to take another I'm going to and if he asks me to take
another after that I'm going to do that and if he puts me into a taxi
and tells the driver to take her easy and steer for the morning I'm
going to let him and if he starts in right away putting it to me in
the cab

I'm not going to whisper
oblivion
do you get me
    not that I'm tired of automats and Childs's and handing out ribbon to
    old ladies that ain't got three teeth and being followed home by pimps
    and stewed guys and sleeping lonely in a whitewashed room three thou-
    sand below Zero   oh no
                    I could stand that
but it's that I'm O Gawd how tired
                                of seeing the white face of you and
                                feeling the old hands of you and
                                being teased and jollied about you
                                and being prayed and implored and
                                bribed and threatened
to give you my beautiful white body
    kiddo
            that's why

                        9

    suppose
    Life is an old man carrying flowers on his head.

    young death sits in a café
    smiling,a piece of money held between
    his thumb and first finger

    (i say "will he buy flowers" to you
    and "Death is young
    life wears velour trousers
    life totters,life has a beard" i

    say to you who are silent.—"Do you see
    Life?he is there and here,

or that,or this
or nothing or an old man 3 thirds
asleep,on his head
flowers,always crying
to nobody something about les
roses les bluets
                    yes,
                        will He buy?
Les belles bottes—oh hear
,pas chères")

and my love slowly answered I think so.   But
I think I see someone else

there is a lady,whose name is Afterwards
she is sitting beside young death,is slender;
likes flowers.

10

it's over a(see just
over this)wall
the apples are(yes
they're gravensteins)all
as red as to lose
and as round as to find.

Each why of a leaf says
(floating each how)
you're which as to die
(each green of a new)
you're who as to grow
but you're he as to do

what must(whispers)be must
be(the wise fool)
if living's to give
so breathing's to steal—
five wishes are five
and one hand is a mind

then over our thief goes
(you go and i)
has pulled(for he's we)
such fruit from what bough
that someone called they
made him pay with his now.

But over a(see just
over this)wall
the red and the round
(they're gravensteins)fall
with kind of a blind
big sound on the ground

| |

Tumbling-hair
        picker of buttercups
                violets
dandelions
And the big bullying daisies
            through the field wonderful
with eyes a little sorry
Another comes
        also picking flowers

in heavenly realms of hellas dwelt
two very different sons of zeus:
one,handsome strong and born to dare
—a fighter to his eyelashes—
the other,cunning ugly lame;
but as you'll shortly comprehend
a marvellous artificer

now Ugly was the husband of
(as happens every now and then
upon a merely human plane)
someone completely beautiful;
and Beautiful,who(truth to sing)
could never quite tell right from wrong,
took brother Fearless by the eyes
and did the deed of joy with him

then Cunning forged a web so subtle
air is comparatively crude;
an indestructible occult
supersnare of resistless metal:
and(stealing toward the blissful pair)
skilfully wafted over them-
selves this implacable unthing

next,our illustrious scientist
petitions the celestial host
to scrutinize his handiwork:
they(summoned by that savage yell
from shining realms of regions dark)
laugh long at Beautiful and Brave
—wildly who rage,vainly who strive;
and being finally released
flee one another like the pest

thus did immortal jealousy
quell divine generosity,

thus reason vanquished instinct and
matter became the slave of mind;
thus virtue triumphed over vice
and beauty bowed to ugliness
and logic thwarted life:and thus—
but look around you,friends and foes

my tragic tale concludes herewith:
soldier,beware of mrs smith

13

now two old ladies sit peacefully knitting,
and their names are sometimes and always

"i can't understand what life could have seen in him" stitch
-counting always severely remarks;and her sister(suppress-
ing a yawn)counters "o i don't know;death's rather attractive"
—"attractive!why how can you say such a thing?when i think
of my poor dear husband"—"now don't be absurd:what i said was
'rather attractive',my dear;and you know very well that
never was very much more than attractive,never was

stunning"(a crash.   Both jump)"good
heavens!" always exclaims "what
was that?"—"well here comes your daughter"
soothes sometimes;at which

death's pretty young wife enters;wringing her hands,and wailing
"that terrible child!"—"what"(sometimes and always together
cry)"now?"—"my doll:my beautiful doll;the very
first doll you gave me,mother(when i could scarcely
walk)with the eyes that opened and shut(you remember:

don't you,auntie;we called her love)and i've treasured
her all these years,and today i went through a closet
looking for something;and opened a box,and there she
lay:and when he saw her,he begged me to let him
hold her;just once:and i told him 'mankind,be careful;
she's terribly fragile:don't break her,or mother'll be angry' "

and then(except for
the clicking of needles)there was silence

14

let us suspect,chérie,this not very big
box completely mysterious,on whose shut
lid in large letters but neatly is
inscribed "Immortality".   And not
go too near it,however people brag
of the wonderful things inside
which are altogether too good to miss—
but we'll go by,together,giving it a wide
berth.   Silently.   Making our feet
think.   Holding our breath—
if we look at it we will want to touch it.
And we mustn't because(something tells me)
ever so very carefully if we
begin to handle it

out jumps Jack Death

X

Urban Glimpses

For a professed devotee of the natural world, Cummings spent a great deal of time in cities, especially New York, which was his home for forty-five years, although he traveled frequently to Paris, Rome, Venice, and other great centers of European culture. Indeed, his anticivilization stance was a self-deceiving pose. He could hardly have existed without the world of art and literature that nurtured him.

Thus, his books are filled with poems reflective of the urban scene, most of them merely descriptive or anecdotal, but he used the material for working up his visual linguistic presentations. His common practice was to keep a personal notebook or diary with him at all times, and he frequently recorded what he encountered on the streets or in the cafés and what he observed of his urban surroundings. Often, after an event had lain mellowing in his notebook for some time, it would emerge as a source for a poem.

In spite of their simplicity, the poems in this section frequently served as a trial for a literary experiment (as the Cummings papers in the Houghton Library make clear), although they do not look as if that were so. "the hours rise

"View from My Room," Hotel Havane, rue St-André-des-Arts,
pencil sketch by E. E. Cummings
Houghton Library, Harvard University

up" was once an exercise in long-lined Whitmanesque free verse, but Cummings later purified it and gave it a dreamlike quality. *"logeorge"* was an early tryout for the ways that spacing on the page could suggest the features of a dialogue and the emotions of speakers. *"i was sitting in mcsorley's"* was written at a time when Cummings was experimenting with sound patterns: he compiled lists of words that have rhyme and consonance—like *dint, grin, point, glint, squint,* and *wink*—or words that begin or end with a group of similar sounds—like *piddle, spittle, topple, wobble, dribble,* and *gobble.* He thought of the work as a sound painting, even though it moved from description into incident (an evil apparition in a saloon). *"stinging"* developed while he was going beyond the influence of the Imagist movement into poems that developed visually.

the hours rise up putting off stars and it is
dawn
into the street of the sky light walks scattering poems

on earth a candle is
extinguished   the city
wakes
with a song upon her
mouth having death in her eyes

and it is dawn
the world
goes forth to murder dreams....

i see in the street where strong
men are digging bread
and i see the brutal faces of
people contented hideous hopeless cruel happy

and it is day,

in the mirror
i see a frail
man
dreaming
dreams
dreams in the mirror

and it
is dusk   on earth

a candle is lighted
and it is dark.
the people are in their houses
the frail man is in his bed
the city

sleeps with death upon her mouth having a song in her eyes
the hours descend,
putting on stars....

in the street of the sky night walks scattering poems

2

but the other
day i was passing a certain
gate,   rain
fell(as it will

in spring)
ropes
of silver gliding from sunny
thunder into freshness

as if god's flowers were
pulling upon bells of
gold   i looked
up

and
thought to myself   Death
and will You with
elaborate fingers possibly touch

the pink hollyhock existence whose
pansy eyes look from morning till
night into the street
unchangingly   the always

old lady always sitting in her
gentle window like
a reminiscence
partaken

softly   at whose gate smile
always the chosen
flowers of reminding

3

logeorge
      lo
           wellifitisn't eddy   how's the boy
grandhave youheard
                shoot

                               you knowjim
goodscout   well

   married

   the hellyousay
           whoto

    'member ritagail
  do i remember rita   what'sthejoke

                         well

                               goddam

don'ttakeit too hard old boy

sayare you kidding   me   because   ifyouare   byhell
easyall george   watchyourstep old fellow

        christ

                that   that

mut

                            4

                the skinny voice

                of the leatherfaced
                woman with the crimson
                nose and coquettishly-
                cocked bonnet

                having ceased   the

                captain
                announces that as three
                dimes seven nickels and ten
                pennies have been deposited upon

                the drum   there is need

of just twenty five cents
dear friends
to make it an even
dollar   whereupon

the Divine Average who was

attracted by the inspired
sister's howling moves
off
will anyone tell him why he should

blow two bits for the coming of Christ Jesus

?
??
???
!

nix,kid

5

a man who had fallen among thieves
lay by the roadside on his back
dressed in fifteenthrate ideas
wearing a round jeer for a hat

fate per a somewhat more than less
emancipated evening
had in return for consciousness
endowed him with a changeless grin

whereon a dozen staunch and leal
citizens did graze at pause
then fired by hypercivic zeal
sought newer pastures or because

swaddled with a frozen brook
of pinkest vomit out of eyes
which noticed nobody he looked
as if he did not care to rise

one hand did nothing on the vest
its wideflung friend clenched weakly dirt
while the mute trouserfly confessed
a button solemnly inert.

Brushing from whom the stiffened puke
i put him all into my arms
and staggered banged with terror through
a million billion trillion stars

6

i was sitting in mcsorley's.   outside it was New York and beauti-
fully snowing.

Inside snug and evil.   the slobbering walls filthily push witless
creases of screaming warmth chuck pillows are noise funnily swallows
swallowing revolvingly pompous a the swallowed mottle with smooth or
a but of rapidly goes gobs the and of flecks of and a chatter sobbings
intersect with which distinct disks of graceful oath,upsoarings the
break on   ceiling-flatness

the Bar.tinking luscious jigs dint of ripe silver with warmlyish
wetflat splurging smells waltz the glush of squirting taps plus slush
of foam knocked off and a faint piddle-of-drops she says I ploc spittle
what the lands thaz me kid in no sir hopping sawdust you kiddo he's a
palping wreaths of badly Yep cigars who jim him why gluey grins topple
together eyes pout gestures stickily point made glints squinting who's
a wink bum-nothing and money fuzzily mouths take big wobbly foot-steps
every goggle cent of it get out ears dribbles soft right old feller
belch the chap hic summore eh chuckles skulch....

and i was sitting in the din thinking drinking the ale,which never
lets you grow old blinking at the low ceiling my being pleasantly was
punctuated by the always retchings of a worthless lamp.

when With a minute terrif   iceffort one dirty squeal of soiling light
yanKing from bushy obscurity a bald greenish foetal head established
It suddenly upon the huge neck around whose unwashed sonorous muscle
the filth of a collar hung gently.

(spattered)by this instant of semiluminous nausea A vast wordless
nondescript genie of trunk trickled firmly in to one exactly-mutilated
ghost of a chair,

a;domeshaped interval of complete plasticity,shoulders,sprouted the
extraordinary arms through an angle of ridiculous velocity commenting
upon an unclean table,and,whose distended immense Both paws slowly
loved a dinted mug

gone Darkness   it was so near to me,i ask of shadow won't you have a
drink?

(the eternal perpetual question)

Inside snugandevil.   i was sitting in mcsorley's   It,did not answer.

outside.(it was New York and beautifully,snowing....

132

that melancholy

fellow'll play
his handorgan
until you say

"i want a fortune"

.At which(smiling)he stops:
& pick
ing up a magical stick
t,a,p,s

this dingy cage:then with a ghost

's rainfaint windthin
voice-which-is
no-voice sobcries

"paw?lee"

—whereupon out(SlO
wLy)steps(to
mount the wand)a by no
means almost

white morethanPerson;who

(riding through space
to diminutive this
opened drawer)tweak

S with his brutebeak

one fatal faded(pinkish or
yellowish maybe)piece
of pitiful paper—
but now,as Mr bowing Cockatoo

proffers the meaning of the stars

14th st dis(because my tears
are full of eyes)appears.   Because
only the truest things always

are true because they can't be true

8

Paris;this April sunset completely utters;
utters serenely silently a cathedral

before whose upward lean magnificent face
the streets turn young with rain,

spiral acres of bloated rose
coiled within cobalt miles of sky
yield to and heed
the mauve
            of twilight(who slenderly descends,
daintily carrying in her eyes the dangerous first stars)
people move love hurry in a gently

arriving gloom and
see!(the new moon
fills abruptly with sudden silver
these torn pockets of lame and begging colour)while
there and here the lithe indolent prostitute
Night,argues

with certain houses

9

stinging
gold swarms
upon the spires
silver

      chants the litanies the
great bells are ringing with rose
the lewd fat bells
                and a tall

wind
is dragging
the
sea

with

dream

-S

A Politician and *A General*, pencil
sketches by E. E. Cummings
Houghton Library,
Harvard University

XI

TARGETS OF SATIRE

CUMMINGS' TEMPERAMENT equipped him well to be a satirist. As his career developed, he made use of all its forms: invective, personal ridicule, burlesque, mimicry, parody, role playing, and verbal irony. In doing so, he employed all kinds of wordplay: puns, circumlocution, slang, dialect, double entendre, misspelling, comic rhyme, and absurd allusion—especially reference to patriotic songs, popular songs, advertising slogans, literary quotations, Latin phrases, proverbs, and nursery rhymes. For example, within a mere four lines, his epigram on Ernest Hemingway employs a number of these devices. The opening line mimics Tennyson's "Cradle Song" from his poem "Sea Dreams": "What does little birdie say/ In her nest at peep of day?" But a stanza from Longfellow's "The Psalm of Life" hovers more maliciously over these lines:

> Life is real! Life is earnest!
> And the grave is not the goal;
> Dust thou art, to dust returnest,
> Was not spoken of the soul.

The bull reference in line three was a reminder of Max East-man's devastating review of Hemingway's *Death in the After-noon* entitled *"Bull in the Afternoon."* The dialect in line three manages to attack Hemingway's masculinity and the message of his recent writing (*Cow thou art, to bull returnest*).

A longer poem such as *"POEM, OR BEAUTY HURTS MR. VINAL"* makes use of a full range of satiric methods in its scatological send-up of the products of most American poets. It even includes an allusive Latin pun when the poets are called *"throstles,"* or song thrushes, the generic name for which is *Turdus musicus.*

The glorification of war with its attendant patriotic postur-ing was a continuing target of Cummings' satire during both world wars. Curiously enough, however, he was also ready to stand up for oppressed nations and denounce the United States for failing to protect them. Russia's attack on Finland in World War II was one occasion, but a more complicated situation arose when Russia invaded Hungary to put down the uprising of 1956. Cummings went into a fuming rage because the U.S. broadcasts over Radio Free Europe had encouraged liberation movements in Eastern Europe but then the U.S. government did nothing to help Hungary—nor did the United Nations in conclave do anything more than offer verbal protests. The result was the poem *"THANKSGIV-ING (1956)."*

Politicians were to Cummings mere salesmen of their pro-grams and ready to stoop to any means for success. All presi-dents of the United States during his adult lifetime, from Wilson to Kennedy, were attacked in one satire or another. An especially hard-hitting example, *"F is for foetus,"* appears here in this section. (The scattered capital letters spell out FDR.)

Given his objections to groupism and collective action in

society, it is no surprise to find Cummings opposed to Communism. But he had special reason for his hatred after his firsthand observation of the soul-smothering effects of the Soviet police state during a trip through Russia (holding a special "without party" visa) in 1931. His diary of this visit, revised to become his book *Eimi,* is his most important prose work and a milestone of political satire.

In the later part of his career, Cummings frequently descended into misanthropic moods that found expression in his poems. The last five poems in this section are representative. His hostility toward social conformity, technological development, and the precedence of mind over heart lies at the base of these works, most of them sonnets and all skillfully adapted to that form. In the mid-twentieth century, there was no need for the Wordsworthian cry to be raised, "Milton! thou should'st be living at this hour."

War

I

a Woman
        of bronze
unhappy
             stands
at the mouth
an oldish woman
                  in a night-gown
           Boosting a

torch
Always
        a tired woman
        she has had children
                  and They have forgotten
        Standing

           looking out
to sea

my sweet old etcetera
aunt lucy during the recent

war could and what
is more did tell you just
what everybody was fighting

for,
my sister

isabel created hundreds
(and
hundreds)of socks not to
mention shirts fleaproof earwarmers

etcetera wristers etcetera,my

mother hoped that

i would die etcetera
bravely of course my father used
to become hoarse talking about how it was
a privilege and if only he
could meanwhile my

self etcetera lay quietly
in the deep mud et

cetera
(dreaming,
et
   cetera,of
Your smile
eyes knees and of your Etcetera)

3

"next to of course god america i
love you land of the pilgrims' and so forth oh
say can you see by the dawn's early my
country 'tis of centuries come and go
and are no more what of it we should worry
in every language even deafanddumb
thy sons acclaim your glorious name by gorry
by jingo by gee by gosh by gum
why talk of beauty what could be more beaut-
iful than these heroic happy dead
who rushed like lions to the roaring slaughter
they did not stop to think they died instead
then shall the voice of liberty be mute?"

He spoke.   And drank rapidly a glass of water

4

i sing of Olaf glad and big
whose warmest heart recoiled at war:
a conscientious object-or

his wellbelovéd colonel(trig
westpointer most succinctly bred)
took erring Olaf soon in hand;
but—though an host of overjoyed
noncoms(first knocking on the head
him)do through icy waters roll
that helplessness which others stroke
with brushes recently employed
anent this muddy toiletbowl,

while kindred intellects evoke
allegiance per blunt instruments—
Olaf(being to all intents
a corpse and wanting any rag
upon what God unto him gave)
responds,without getting annoyed
"I will not kiss your fucking flag"

straightway the silver bird looked grave
(departing hurriedly to shave)

but—though all kinds of officers
(a yearning nation's blueeyed pride)
their passive prey did kick and curse
until for wear their clarion
voices and boots were much the worse,
and egged the firstclassprivates on
his rectum wickedly to tease
by means of skilfully applied
bayonets roasted hot with heat—
Olaf(upon what were once knees)
does almost ceaselessly repeat
"there is some shit I will not eat"

our president,being of which
assertions duly notified
threw the yellowsonofabitch
into a dungeon,where he died

Christ(of His mercy infinite)
i pray to see;and Olaf,too

preponderatingly because
unless statistics lie he was
more brave than me:more blond than you.

ygUDuh

    ydoan
    yunnuhstan

    ydoan o
    yunnuhstan dem
    yguduh ged

        yunnuhstan dem doidee
        yguduh ged riduh
        ydoan o nudn
LISN bud LISN

        dem
        gud
        am

        lidl yelluh bas
        tuds weer goin

duhSIVILEYEzum

plato told

him:he couldn't
believe it(jesus

told him;he
wouldn't believe
it)lao

tsze
certainly told
him,and general
(yes

mam)
sherman;
and even
(believe it
or

not)you
told him:i told
him;we told him
(he didn't believe it,no

sir)it took
a nipponized bit of
the old sixth

avenue
el;in the top of his head:to tell

him

Politics

I

F is for foetus(a

punkslapping
mobsucking
gravypissing poppa but
who just couldn't help it no

matter how hard he never tried)the

great pink
superme
diocri
ty of

a hyperhypocritical D

mocra
c(sing
down with the fascist beast
boom

boom)two eyes

for an eye four
teeth for a tooth
(and the wholly babble open at
blessed are the peacemuckers)

$ $ $ etc(as

the boodle's bent is the
crowd inclined it's

freedom from freedom
the common man wants)

honey swoRkey mollypants

2

a salesman is an it that stinks Excuse

Me whether it's president of the you were say
or a jennelman name misder finger isn't
important whether it's millions of other punks
or just a handful absolutely doesn't
matter and whether it's in lonjewray

or shrouds is immaterial it stinks

a salesman is an it that stinks to please

but whether to please itself or someone else
makes no more difference than if it sells
hate condoms education snakeoil vac
uumcleaners terror strawberries democ
ra(caveat emptor)cy superfluous hair

or Think We've Met subhuman rights Before

3

the way to hump a cow is not
to get yourself a stool
but draw a line around the spot
and call it beautifool

to multiply because and why
dividing thens by nows
and adding and(i understand)
is hows to hump a cows

the way to hump a cow is not
to elevate your tool
but drop a penny in the slot
and bellow like a bool

to lay a wreath from ancient greath
on insulated brows
(while tossing boms at uncle toms)
is hows to hump a cows

the way to hump a cow is not
to push and then to pull
but practicing the art of swot
to preach the golden rull

to vote for me(all decent mem
and wonens will allows
which if they don't to hell with them)
is hows to hump a cows

Communism and Fascism

I

(of Ever-Ever Land i speak
sweet morons gather roun'
who does not dare to stand or sit
may take it lying down)

down with the human soul
and anything else uncanned
for everyone carries canopeners
in Ever-Ever Land

(for Ever-Ever Land is a place
that's as simple as simple can be
and was built that way on purpose
by simple people like we)

down with hell and heaven
and all the religious fuss
infinity pleased our parents
one inch looks good to us

(and Ever-Ever Land is a place
that's measured and safe and known
where it's lucky to be unlucky
and the hitler lies down with the cohn)

down above all with love
and everything perverse
or which makes some feel more better
when all ought to feel less worse

(but only sameness is normal
in Ever-Ever Land
for a bad cigar is a woman
but a gland is only a gland)

2

kumrads die because they're told)
kumrads die before they're old
(kumrads aren't afraid to die
kumrads don't
and kumrads won't
believe in life)and death knows whie

(all good kumrads you can tell
by their altruistic smell
moscow pipes good kumrads dance)
kumrads enjoy
s.freud knows whoy
the hope that you may mess your pance

every kumrad is a bit
of quite unmitigated hate
(travelling in a futile groove
god knows why)
and so do i
(because they are afraid to love

3

red-rag and pink-flag
blackshirt and brown
strut-mince and stink-brag
have all come to town

some like it shot
and some like it hung
and some like it in the twot
nine months young

4

THANKSGIVING (1956)

a monstering horror swallows
this unworld me by you
as the god of our fathers' fathers bows
to a which that walks like a who

but the voice-with-a-smile of democracy
announces night & day
"all poor little peoples that want to be free
just trust in the u s a"

suddenly uprose hungary
and she gave a terrible cry
"no slave's unlife shall murder me
for i will freely die"

she cried so high thermopylae
heard her and marathon
and all prehuman history
and finally The UN

"be quiet little hungary
and do as you are bid
a good kind bear is angary
we fear for the quo pro quid"

uncle sam shrugs his pretty
pink shoulders you know how
and he twitches a liberal titty
and lisps "i'm busy right now"

so rah-rah-rah democracy
let's all be as thankful as hell
and bury the statue of liberty
(because it begins to smell)

The Literary Scene

I

POEM,OR BEAUTY HURTS MR.VINAL

take it from me kiddo
believe me
my country,'tis of

you,land of the Cluett
Shirt Boston Garter and Spearmint
Girl With The Wrigley Eyes(of you
land of the Arrow Ide
and Earl &
Wilson
Collars)of you i
sing:land of Abraham Lincoln and Lydia E. Pinkham,
land above all of Just Add Hot Water And Serve—
from every B.V.D.

let freedom ring

amen.   i do however protest,anent the un
-spontaneous and otherwise scented merde which
greets one(Everywhere Why)as divine poesy per
that and this radically defunct periodical.   i would

suggest that certain ideas gestures
rhymes,like Gillette Razor Blades
having been used and reused
to the mystical moment of dullness emphatically are
Not To Be Resharpened.   (Case in point

if we are to believe these gently O sweetly
melancholy trillers amid the thrillers
these crepuscular violinists among my and your
skyscrapers—Helen & Cleopatra were Just Too Lovely,

The Snail's On The Thorn enter Morn and God's
In His andsoforth

do you get me?)according
to such supposedly indigenous
throstles Art is O World O Life
a formula:example,Turn Your Shirttails Into
Drawers and If It Isn't An Eastman It Isn't A
Kodak therefore my friends let
us now sing each and all fortissimo A-
mer
i

ca,I
love,
You.   And there're a
hun-dred-mil-lion-oth-ers,like
all of you successfully if
delicately gelded(or spaded)
gentlemen(and ladies)—pretty

littleliverpill-
hearted-Nujolneeding-There's-A-Reason
americans(who tensetendoned and with
upward vacant eyes,painfully
perpetually crouched,quivering,upon the
sternly allotted sandpile
—how silently
emit a tiny violetflavoured nuisance:Odor?

ono.
comes out like a ribbon lies flat on the brush

2

what does little Ernest croon
in his death at afternoon?
(kow dow r 2 bul retoinis
wus de woids uf lil Oinis

3

flotsam and jetsam
are gentlemen poeds
urseappeal netsam
our spinsters and coeds)

thoroughly bretish
they scout the inhuman
itarian fetish
that man isn't wuman

vive the millenni
um three cheers for labor
give all things to enni
one bugger thy nabor

(neck and senecktie
are gentlemen ppoyds
even whose recktie
are covered by lloyd's

4

BALLAD OF AN INTELLECTUAL

Listen,you morons great and small
to the tale of an intellectuall
(and if you don't profit by his career
don't ever say Hoover gave nobody beer).

'Tis frequently stated out where he was born
that a rose is as weak as its shortest thorn:
they spit like quarters and sleep in their boots
and anyone dies when somebody shoots
and the sheriff arrives after everyone's went;
which isn't,perhaps,an environment
where you would(and I should)expect to find
overwhelming devotion to things of the mind.
But when it rains chickens we'll all catch larks
—to borrow a phrase from Karl the Marks.

As a child he was puny;shrank from noise
hated the girls and mistrusted the boise,
didn't like whisky,learned to spell
and generally seemed to be going to hell;
so his parents,encouraged by desperation,
gave him a classical education
(and went to sleep in their boots again
out in the land where women are main).

You know the rest:a critic of note,
a serious thinker,a lyrical pote,
lectured on Art from west to east
—did sass-seyeity fall for it? Cheast!
if a dowager balked at our hero's verse
he'd knock her cold with a page from Jerse;
why,he used to say to his friends,he used
"for getting a debutante give me Prused"
and many's the heiress who's up and swooned

after one canto by Ezra Pooned
(or—to borrow a cadence from Karl the Marx—
a biting chipmunk never barx).

But every bathtub will have its gin
and one man's sister's another man's sin
and a hand in the bush is a stitch in time
and Aint It All A Bloody Shime
and he suffered a fate which is worse than death
and I don't allude to unpleasant breath.

Our blooming hero awoke,one day,
to find he had nothing whatever to say:
which I might interpret(just for fun)
as meaning the es of a be was dun
and I mightn't think(and you mightn't,too)
that a Five Year Plan's worth a Gay Pay Oo
and both of us might irretrievably pause
ere believing that Stalin is Santa Clause:
which happily proves that neither of us
is really an intellectual cus.

For what did our intellectual do,
when he found himself so empty and blo?
he pondered a while and he said,said he
"It's the social system,it isn't me!
Not I am a fake,but America's phoney!
Not I am no artist,but Art's bologney!
Or—briefly to paraphrase Karl the Marx—
'The first law of nature is,trees will be parx.' "

Now all you morons of sundry classes
(who read the Times and who buy the Masses)
if you don't profit by his career
don't ever say Hoover gave nobody beer.

For whoso conniveth at Lenin his dream
shall dine upon bayonets,isn't and seam

and a miss is as good as a mile is best
for if you're not bourgeois you're Eddie Gest
and wastelands live and waistlines die,
which I very much hope it won't happen to eye;
or as comrade Shakespeare remarked of old
All that Glisters Is Mike Gold

(but a rolling snowball gathers no sparks
—and the same hold true of Karl the Marks).

Misanthropic Moods

I

when serpents bargain for the right to squirm
and the sun strikes to gain a living wage—
when thorns regard their roses with alarm
and rainbows are insured against old age

when every thrush may sing no new moon in
if all screech-owls have not okayed his voice
—and any wave signs on the dotted line
or else an ocean is compelled to close

when the oak begs permission of the birch
to make an acorn—valleys accuse their
mountains of having altitude—and march
denounces april as a saboteur

then we'll believe in that incredible
unanimal mankind(and not until)

2

pity this busy monster,manunkind,

not.   Progress is a comfortable disease:
your victim(death and life safely beyond)

plays with the bigness of his littleness
—electrons deify one razorblade
into a mountainrange;lenses extend

unwish through curving wherewhen till unwish
returns on its unself.
                                    A world of made
is not a world of born—pity poor flesh

and trees,poor stars and stones,but never this
fine specimen of hypermagical

ultraomnipotence.   We doctors know

a hopeless case if—listen:there's a hell
of a good universe next door;let's go

3

Space being(don't forget to remember)Curved
(and that reminds me who said o yes Frost
Something there is which isn't fond of walls)

an electromagnetic(now I've lost
the)Einstein expanded Newton's law preserved
conTinuum(but we read that beFore)

of Course life being just a Reflex you
know since Everything is Relative or

to sum it All Up god being Dead(not to

mention inTerred)
                                    LONG LIVE that Upwardlooking
Serene Illustrious and Beatific
Lord of Creation,MAN:

at a least crooking
of Whose compassionate digit,earth's most terrific

quadruped swoons into billiardBalls!

4

("fire stop thief help murder save the world"

what world?
            is it themselves these insects mean?
when microscopic shriekings shall have snarled
threads of celestial silence huger than
eternity,men will be saviours
                          —flop
grasshopper,exactly nothing's soon;
scream,all ye screamers,till your if is up
and vanish under prodigies of un)

"have you" the mountain,while his maples wept
air to blood,asked "something a little child
who's just as small as me can do or be?"
god whispered him a snowflake "yes:you may
sleep now,my mountain" and this mountain slept

while his pines lifted their green lives and smiled

5

Jehovah buried,Satan dead,
do fearers worship Much and Quick;
badness not being felt as bad,
itself thinks goodness what is meek;
obey says toc,submit says tic,
Eternity's a Five Year Plan:
if Joy with Pain shall hang in hock
who dares to call himself a man?

go dreamless knaves on Shadows fed,
your Harry's Tom,your Tom is Dick;
while Gadgets murder squawk and add,
the cult of Same is all the chic;
by instruments,both span and spic,
are justly measured Spic and Span:
to kiss the mike if Jew turn kike
who dares to call himself a man?

loudly for Truth have liars pled,
their heels for Freedom slaves will click;
where Boobs are holy,poets mad,
illustrious punks of Progress shriek;
when Souls are outlawed,Hearts are sick,
Hearts being sick,Minds nothing can:
if Hate's a game and Love's a fuck
who dares to call himself a man?

King Christ,this world is all aleak;
and lifepreservers there are none:
and waves which only He may walk
Who dares to call Himself a man.

Paris: Notre Dame, pencil sketch by E. E. Cummings
Houghton Library, Harvard University

XII

ENDINGS

TOWARD THE END of life, E. E. Cummings was considerably sobered by the aches and stresses of aging. He suffered severely from arthritis and was forced to wear a metal-braced corset that he called "The Iron Maiden." Other ills and physical deteriorations caused him additional discomfort and, on two occasions, surgery. The decline in his physical condition probably accounts for the increasing harshness in his satires and his readiness, like Mark Twain in his last years, to denounce the human race. But it also brought him to recognize, from time to time, that he shared with other human beings the inclination to selfish behavior and unjustified criticism of others. Thus, poems begin to crop up that acknowledge his own faults. They usually express a divided view of human nature, that human beings are half angel and half demon—as he expressed it in the poems "so many selves(so many fiends and gods" and "no man,if men are gods."

This is a long-standing Christian concept, and indeed Cummings turned toward religion in his later years. "As I grow older, I tend toward piety," he acknowledged one Christmas season in 1948. His journals contain occasional wrestlings with religious belief and a great many prayers to "le bon Dieu." Poems like "i thank You God for most this amazing" and "i am a little church" are much in keeping with this turn of mind. But his reading also extended into Hinduism, Zen Buddhism, and Taoism, which appealed to a mystical tendency in Cummings that was quite congruent with his long-time interest in Emerson and New England Transcendentalism. Thus, his religious outlook continued to return to the Unitarianism of his father, an undogmatic position, which nevertheless held a concept of God as omnipresent in the natural world who, although incomprehensible to the understanding of ordinary mortals, was most closely approached by being in tune with nature.

Cummings' poems about the end of life show his acceptance of being a part of the natural process, which becomes, at length, dissolution into the "mystery to be." There are some expressions of regret about the loss of powers in old age—to have to make do with "contentment" rather than "ecstasy" and to substitute "caution" for "curiosity," as he says in the poem "for prodigal read generous." But the optimism that colored his early life surrounds his contemplations of death and afterlife, as we can observe when he says (in "all nearness pauses,while a star can grow") "if a world ends/ more than all worlds begin to(see?)begin," or when he envisions himself finally lying down "to dream of Spring."

Self-Excoriation

I

a total stranger one black day
knocked living the hell out of me—

who found forgiveness hard because
my(as it happened)self he was

—but now that fiend and i are such
immortal friends the other's each

2

so many selves(so many fiends and gods
each greedier than every)is a man
(so easily one in another hides;
yet man can,being all,escape from none)

so huge a tumult is the simplest wish:
so pitiless a massacre the hope
most innocent(so deep's the mind of flesh
and so awake what waking calls asleep)

so never is most lonely man alone
(his briefest breathing lives some planet's year,
his longest life's a heartbeat of some sun;
his least unmotion roams the youngest star)

—how should a fool that calls him "I" presume
to comprehend not numerable whom?

3

no man,if men are gods;but if gods must
be men,the sometimes only man is this
(most common,for each anguish is his grief;
and,for his joy is more than joy,most rare)

a fiend,if fiends speak truth;if angels burn

by their own generous completely light,
an angel;or(as various worlds he'll spurn
rather than fail immeasurable fate)
coward,clown,traitor,idiot,dreamer,beast—

such was a poet and shall be and is

—who'll solve the depths of horror to defend
a sunbeam's architecture with his life:
and carve immortal jungles of despair
to hold a mountain's heartbeat in his hand

Religious Leanings

1

i thank You God for most this amazing
day:for the leaping greenly spirits of trees
and a blue true dream of sky;and for everything
which is natural which is infinite which is yes

(i who have died am alive again today,
and this is the sun's birthday;this is the birth
day of life and of love and wings:and of the gay
great happening illimitably earth)

how should tasting touching hearing seeing
breathing any—lifted from the no
of all nothing—human merely being
doubt unimaginable You?

(now the ears of my ears awake and
now the eyes of my eyes are opened)

2

i am a little church(no great cathedral)
far from the splendor and squalor of hurrying cities
—i do not worry if briefer days grow briefest,
i am not sorry when sun and rain make april

my life is the life of the reaper and the sower;
my prayers are prayers of earth's own clumsily striving
(finding and losing and laughing and crying)children
whose any sadness or joy is my grief or my gladness

around me surges a miracle of unceasing
birth and glory and death and resurrection:
over my sleeping self float flaming symbols
of hope,and i wake to a perfect patience of mountains

i am a little church(far from the frantic
world with its rapture and anguish)at peace with nature
—i do not worry if longer nights grow longest;
i am not sorry when silence becomes singing

winter by spring,i lift my diminutive spire to
merciful Him Whose only now is forever:
standing erect in the deathless truth of His presence
(welcoming humbly His light and proudly His darkness)

3

it is winter a moon in the afternoon
and warm air turning into January darkness up
through which sprouting gently,the cathedral
leans its dreamy spine against thick sunset

i perceive in front of our lady a ring of people
a brittle swoon of centrifugally expecting
faces clumsily which devours a man,three cats,
five white mice,and a baboon.

O a monkey with a sharp face waddling carefully
the length of this padded pole;a monkey attached
by a chain securely to this always talking
individual,mysterious witty hatless.

Cats which move smoothly from neck to neck of bottles,cats
smoothly willowing out and in between bottles,who step smoothly
and rapidly along this pole over five squirming
mice;or leap through hoops of fire,creating smoothness.

People stare,the drunker applaud
while twilight takes the sting out of the vermilion
jacket of nodding hairy Jacqueline who is given a mouse
to hold lovingly,

our lady what do you think of this?   Do your proud fingers and
your arms tremble remembering something squirming fragile
and which had been presented unto you by a mystery?
...the cathedral recedes into weather without answering

4

from spiralling ecstatically this

proud nowhere of earth's most prodigious night
blossoms a newborn babe:around him,eyes
—gifted with every keener appetite
than mere unmiracle can quite appease—
humbly in their imagined bodies kneel
(over time space doom dream while floats the whole

perhapsless mystery of paradise)

mind without soul may blast some universe
to might have been,and stop ten thousand stars
but not one heartbeat of this child;nor shall
even prevail a million questionings
against the silence of his mother's smile

—whose only secret all creation sings

brIght

bRight s??? big
(soft)

soft near calm
(Bright)
calm st?? holy

(soft briGht deep)
yeS near sta? calm star big yEs
alone
(wHo

Yes
near deep whO big alone soft near
deep calm deep
????Ht ?????T)
Who(holy alone)holy(alone holy)alone

Whispers of Mortality

I

old age sticks
up Keep
Off
signs)&

youth yanks them
down(old
age
cries No

Tres)&(pas)
youth laughs
(sing
old age

scolds Forbid
den Stop
Must
n't Don't

&)youth goes
right on
gr
owing old

2

for prodigal read generous
—for youth read age—
read for sheer wonder mere surprise
(then turn the page)

contentment read for ecstasy
—for poem prose—
caution for curiosity
(and close your eyes)

3

enter no(silence is the blood whose flesh
is singing)silence:but unsinging.   In
spectral such hugest how hush,one

dead leaf stirring makes a crash

—far away(as far as alive)lies
april;and i breathe-move-and-seem some
perpetually roaming whylessness—

autumn has gone:will winter never come?

o come,terrible anonymity;enfold
phantom me with the murdering minus of cold
—open this ghost with millionary knives of wind—
scatter his nothing all over what angry skies and

gently
        (very whiteness:absolute peace,
never imaginable mystery)
                                descend

4

now does our world descend
the path to nothingness
(cruel now cancels kind;
friends turn to enemies)
therefore lament,my dream
and don a doer's doom

create is now contrive;
imagined,merely know
(freedom:what makes a slave)
therefore,my life,lie down
and more by most endure
all that you never were

hide,poor dishonoured mind
who thought yourself so wise;
and much could understand
concerning no and yes:
if they've become the same
it's time you unbecame

where climbing was and bright
is darkness and to fall
(now wrong's the only right
since brave are cowards all)
therefore despair,my heart
and die into the dirt

but from this endless end
of briefer each our bliss—
where seeing eyes go blind
(where lips forget to kiss)
where everything's nothing
—arise,my soul;and sing

all nearness pauses,while a star can grow

all distance breathes a final dream of bells;
perfectly outlined against afterglow
are all amazing the and peaceful hills

(not where not here but neither's blue most both)

and history immeasurably is
wealthier by a single sweet day's death:
as not imagined secrecies comprise

goldenly huge whole the upfloating moon.

Time's a strange fellow;
                        more he gives than takes
(and he takes all)nor any marvel finds
quite disappearance but some keener makes
losing,gaining
                        —love! if a world ends

more than all worlds begin to(see?)begin

6

        what is
        a
        voyage

        ?

        up
        upup:go
        ing

downdowndown

com;ing won
der
ful sun

moon stars the all,& a

(big
ger than
big

gest could even

begin to be)dream
of;a thing:of
a creature who's

O

cean
(everywhere
nothing

but light and dark;but

never forever
& when)un
til one strict

here of amazing most

now,with what
thousands of(hundreds
of)millions of

CriesWhichAreWings

when life is quite through with
and leaves say alas,
much is to do
for the swallow,that closes
a flight in the blue;

when love's had his tears out,
perhaps shall pass
a million years
(while a bee dozes
on the poppies,the dears;

when all's done and said,and
under the grass
lies her head
by oaks and roses
deliberated.)

8

in time of daffodils(who know
the goal of living is to grow)
forgetting why,remember how

in time of lilacs who proclaim
the aim of waking is to dream,
remember so(forgetting seem)

in time of roses(who amaze
our now and here with paradise)
forgetting if,remember yes

in time of all sweet things beyond
whatever mind may comprehend,
remember seek(forgetting find)

and in a mystery to be
(when time from time shall set us free)
forgetting me,remember me

9

Now i lay(with everywhere around)
me(the great dim deep sound
of rain;and of always and of nowhere)and

what a gently welcoming darkestness—

now i lay me down(in a most steep
more than music)feeling that sunlight is
(life and day are)only loaned:whereas
night is given(night and death and the rain

are given;and given is how beautifully snow)

now i lay me down to dream of(nothing
i or any somebody or you
can begin to begin to imagine)

something which nobody may keep.
now i lay me down to dream of Spring

one

t
hi
s

snowflake

(a
  li
    ght
  in
g)

is upon a gra

v
es
t

one

Twilight Moon: Assisi from a private collection

POSTLUDE

life is more true than reason will deceive
(more secret or than madness did reveal)
deeper is life than lose:higher than have
—but beauty is more each than living's all

multiplied with infinity sans if
the mightiest meditations of mankind
cancelled are by one merely opening leaf
(beyond whose nearness there is no beyond)

or does some littler bird than eyes can learn
look up to silence and completely sing?
futures are obsolete;pasts are unborn
(here less than nothing's more than everything)

death,as men call him,ends what they call men
—but beauty is more now than dying's when

INDEX OF TITLES
and Dates of Publication